Excel Formulas and Functions

Step-By-Step Guide with Examples

Table of Contents

Introduction

For many of us, Excel is nothing more than a basic spreadsheet, something we may use on the odd occasion, but for some, it is part of our daily lives. Microsoft Excel is more than just a spreadsheet; it is an essential tool for businesses. In fact, it would be fair to say that it is probably one of the most important tools that a business could have at its disposal. Some of the best uses for Excel include extracting data into charts, using it to identify problems and trends, bringing all the data together from multiple files and other sources so it's all in one easy-to-use place and much more.

The basis of Excel lies in formulas and functions, used for storing data and retrieving it, for doing calculations, and for analyzing data, all in one simple grid format. It is these formulas and functions that provide the biggest headaches for inexperienced users and that is what my guide is all about – how to use them and a look at some of the most commonly used ones. Given that there are more than 400 functions alone and not much less in the way of formulas, I couldn't possibly go over every single one of them. You don't need to know them all though; Excel has a built-in Function Wizard that helps you to get the best function for what you are doing and built-in Formula Intellisense helps with formulas.

I am assuming that you have some basic knowledge of Excel that you know how to open a workbook, change sheets, and input data for example. If not, you need to familiarize yourself with Excel before we begin. You will also need to be using Excel 2013 or higher for this guide.

Without further ado, let's immerse ourselves in the world of Excel formulas and functions.

Formulas and Functions – The Basics

Before we go into any of the functions or formulas, there are two key terms that you need to be aware of:

- **Formula** – an expression that is used for calculating the value of one or more cells. For example, =B1+B2+B3+B4 is the formula we would use for adding the values in the cells B1 through to B4.
- **Function** – these are formulas that have already been defined in Excel and they are used for carrying out calculations in a specific order, based on specific values which are called 'parameters' or 'arguments.' For example, rather than telling Excel that you want to add each value like we did in the example above with formulas, a function called SUM can be used to add an entire range of values: =SUM(B1:B4)

Open a new Excel workbook and look at the top, at the 'ribbon' as it is known. You will see various options, including 'File,' 'Home,' 'Insert,' etc. You will see an option for 'Formulas'; click on this to see all the functions that are built-in and stored in the Function Library. As I mentioned at the start of the guide, there are more than 400 of these functions, but you can use the Function Wizard to help you. You will find this in the Formula tab; just click on the first option called 'Insert Function.' Here you will see all the functions, simply click the one you want to use. And, when you type in = (function name) into any cell, Intellisense will automatically input the correct syntax and the correct arguments.

All formulas must be preceded by a = (equal) sign, followed by the name of the function and then a set of brackets to include any arguments. One more tip; type in the name of a function and click on it – it will automatically become a hyperlink that you can click on, opening the built-in Help topic for the function.

Lastly, although all function names are in capital letters, you do not need to type them in this way – Excel will automatically convert the name to capitals for you once you have completed the formula and tapped the Enter key on your keyboard.

That is the basics for you so, without wasting any more time, these are some of the most common Excel functions along with examples of formulas.

Relative and Absolute Cell References

Before we get into the functions and the formulas, you need to be aware of cell references, in particular, absolute and relative references. Why? When you come to copy a formula with cell references in it, you might find that the references change.

If you were to copy a specific formula two rows to the left, the cell references inside that formula would move two cells to the left. If you copy a formula four rows down and two rows right, the references will move three down and two right. That is because the references in the formula are 'relative' references – they will change relative to wherever the formula is copied to.

If you don't want this to happen, you need to make your cell references 'absolute.' To do this, all you do is insert a dollar sign ($) before the letter of the column or the row. For example:

$D$4

This refers to cell D4 and until you copy the formula, you will see no difference in how $D$4 and D4 work. When you copy a formula with $ in it, the references will not change, no matter where you copy it to.

NOTE – When you are typing your formulas in, pressing F4 immediately you enter a cell reference will toggle between relative and absolute.

The real trick to successful spreadsheets is in making a decision before you copy any formula, which of the references included are to be relative and which are to be absolute. Let's look into both a little deeper so you know which one to use:

Relative References

Relative references are used the most in Excel formulas. They are simple, basic references that will change as and when you copy them when you use the Autofill feature.

For example:

Input the following formula into a cell on an Excel worksheet

+SUM(C6:C9)

Copy it to the next cell across and look at the formula. You will see it has changed to:

=SUM(D6:D9)

Absolute References

Sometimes, you will come across a situation in which the cell reference needs to remain exactly the same when you copy it or use Autofill. As explained above, you need to insert the dollar sign ($) to hold the row or the column reference constant.

For example:

Imagine that you are trying to calculate the commission due to each of your sales staff. When you copy the cell with the references in it, in our case, C10, you do not want the references to change, no matter how many times you copy it. You need the row and the column to stay exactly the same because, no matter where the formula is on the sheet, it must still refer to cell C10. SO, when you write your cell reference, you would write it like this:

$C$10

Now the cell references will remain absolute, i.e., it doesn't change.

Absolute Cell Reference Summary

These are the uses for the absolute cell references:

- $B1 – changes the row reference, while the column reference will remain the same
- B$1 – changes the column reference, while the row reference remains the same
- $B$1 – will not change either the row or the column reference

Take a Shortcut

When you are putting absolute cell references into a formula, there is a quick and easy way to do it. After the cell reference has been typed in, press the F4 key. Excel will now go through each of the possibilities you can use so, keep pressing F4 until you get the right one.

For example:

You could type in

=C5*$C$10

Or, you could have typed in

=C5*C10

And then pressed F4 so that C10 changes to $C$10. If you continue to press on F4, you will see it change to C$10, $C10 and lastly just plain C10. The F4 key will only change the reference that is immediately to the left of the point of insertion.

SUM

The very first function, the most common one that you need to learn is SUM. This is the function that does basic addition operations:

=SUM(number1, [number2], ...)

That is the syntax for the SUM function and, in every function that you write, arguments inside round parentheses – () – are required, while any optional arguments must be placed inside a set of square brackets – []. Any formula using SUM must have a minimum of 1 number, referencing one or more cells. For example:

=SUM(B2:B6)

This will add the values inside cells B2 through B6

=SUM(B3, B6)

This will add the values in B2 and B6 together

=SUM(B2:B6)/4

This will add the values inside B2 through B6 and will then divide the answer by 4

How to Use SUM for Simple Calculations

If you wanted to total several values in different cells quickly, Excel can be used as a calculator. All you need to do is use the addition operator (+) just as you would add numbers on a calculator, like this:

=4+5+6

OR

=A2+B4+C7

However, if you were in the position of needing to add dozens or hundreds of rows together, it would be cumbersome to reference every single cell. Instead, the SUM function will do it all for you.

The SUM function can take up to a maximum of 255 numbers in any single formula. Each argument may be a negative or positive number and it may be a single value, cell or a range of values. For example:

=SUM(B1:B100)

=SUM(B1, B2, B5)

=SUM(2, 7, -4)

To use SUM to add values that are in different ranges or to combine 2 or more numeric values, you would do this:

=SUM(B2:B4, B8:B9)

=SUM(B2:B6, B9, 10)

In the real world, the SUM function tends to get used in large formulas and as part of calculations that are a bit more complex. For example, SUM could be added to the IF function (more about this in a later chapter), in the argument 'value_if_true'. To add up the values in the columns A, B, and C, provided that every cell in the row that is in the formula has a value. If not, a warning message is displayed:

=IF(AND($A2<"", $B2<>"", $C2<>""), SUM($A2:$C2), "Value missing")

Using AUTOSUM

What if you wanted to add one range of numbers, either a column, a row or adjacent ones, Excel will do the right formula for you. All you need to do is click on the cell beside the values that you want added, click on Home>Edit on the ribbon and then click on AUTOSUM. Hit the Enter key and a SUM formula gets automatically entered for you.

Summing a Column

As well as automatically giving you the formula, AUTOSUM will also choose the range of cells that you most likely to want to add up. Most of the time, Excel does this alright but, on the occasion when it doesn't, you can change the range manually. To do this, click on the cell that contains the range to be added.

Type in =SUM(

Click on the first cell to be included in the range and then, keeping your mouse button pressed, drag down to the last cell in the range. Press the Enter key and the correct range is included.

TIP – A quick way of using AUTOSUM is to use a shortcut. Press the ALT key down on your keyboard, type = and hit the Enter key – the formula will be automatically entered.

AUTOSUM isn't just for adding up values though; it can also be used for entering the following functions, all of which will be covered in this guide:

- AVERAGE
- COUNT
- MIN
- MAX

This function does what it says on the tin – it finds the mean or average of a series of numbers. The syntax for AVERAGE is much like that of SUM:

=AVERAGE(number1, [number 2], ...)

Number1 and number 2, right up to however many you include, are the values that you are finding the average from. The argument, 'number1', is a requirement but, as with SUM, anything inside the [] is optional and you can add in up to 255 of these arguments in one formula. You may supply the arguments as cell references, ranges or individual numbers.

Calculating an Average

To calculate the average of a specific set of numbers, you can put those numbers straight into the formula:

=AVERAGE(2,3,4,5)

The returned result from this will be 3.5.

If you wanted to calculate the average of a column, you would need to supply the column reference:

=AVERAGE(B:B)

And, to get an average of a row, you would need to put in the row reference:

=AVERAGE(2:B)

If you wanted to get the average from a specific range, you would need to input that range into the formula:

=AVERAGE(B1:D30)

If you want to get the average from a range of cells that are not adjacent to one another, you must input each cell reference:

=AVERAGE(A2, B10, C12, D39)

You can include any cell reference or any range in one formula as required. For example, you could calculate the average of 3 ranges and 2 single cells:

=AVERAGE(A3:A5, B7:B9, C2:C11, A23, B13)

TIP – To round up the returned result to the closest integer, you can use the ROUND function in Excel:

=AVERAGE(A3:A5, B7:B9, C2:C11, A23, B13), 0)

COUNT and COUNTA

If you wanted to know how many cells contain a numeric value, which is either a date or a number, in a range of cells, you would use the COUNT function, the syntax of which is:

=COUNT(value1, [value2], …)

Value1 and value 2, along with any other value you choose to add, are the ranges or the references that you want to find all the numeric values from. You can add up to 255 arguments to each formula. Here's an example of finding the numeric cells in a range:

=COUNT(B1:B100)

NOTE - Because Excel stores dates as serial numbers, the COUNT function will include dates, times and numbers.

These are the rules that COUNT function works by:

- If the arguments used in the COUNT formula are individual cell references or ranges, COUNT will only look for dates, numbers and times, nothing else. If a cell is blank or it contains anything other than a numeric value, it will be ignored.
- If you input values straight into the arguments for COUNT, the function will count the usual, dates, numbers and times, and it will also count a text representation of a number, for example, a number surrounded by quotation marks, like "7", and it will count TRUE and FALSE, both Boolean values.

Have a look at this example:

=COUNT(2, "bananas", "4", 2/2/2018, FALSE)

How many cells contain numeric values? The answer returned will be 4 because COUNT will count:

2

"4"

2/2/2018

FALSE

COUNTA

The COUNTA function will count any cell that has a value, regardless of what that value is, and will ignore any blank cells. The syntax is similar to COUNT:

=COUNTA(value1, [value2], ...)

Again, the values are the individual cells or ranges where you want to find the number of cells with a value.

For example, using COUNTA on a range:

=COUNTA(B1:B100)

If you wanted to find all the cells with a value in ranges that are not adjacent to one another, you would do this:

=COUNTA(A1:A11, B1:B20, C1:C30)

As you should be able to see here, you do not need to supply ranges of equal size – they can all have different numbers of columns and rows.

Don't forget, COUNT will only count those cells with a numerical value in them, while COUNTA looks for all the cells with any value in them, including:

- Numbers
- Dates

- Times
- Text value
- Boolean TRUE
- Boolean FALSE
- Error values, such as #N/A or #VALUE
- Text strings that are empty ("")

Sometimes, the result that you get from COUNTA may not be what you see with your eyes. COUNTA may include cells that, visually, look empty but may not be. For example, if you were to put a space into a cell, it would be counted. Or, of the cell had a formula in it that resulted in an empty string, that cell would also be counted. In short, COUNTA will only ignore cells that are totally empty.

IF

The IF function is incredibly useful and one of the more popular. It is used for testing conditions and, should the condition be met, it will return a value. A different value is returned if the condition isn't met. Anyone who is familiar with basic computer programming languages will already have come across this.

IF is a logical function and it returns only Boolean values – TRUE or FALSE. The syntax is:

=IF(logical_test, [value_if_true], [value_if_false])

As you can see from the syntax, there are 3 arguments in the IF function, but the first is the only required one; the others are optional, as you can see by the square brackets that surround them [].

The first argument, logical test, is a logical expression or a value that may be TRUE or it may be FALSE. This argument can be a text value, number, date, or any of the comparison operators.

For example, you could express the logical test as:

A1="sold"

OR

A1<12/1/2018, A1=10

OR

A1>10.

The expression, value_if_true, will return the value when the test condition has been met, i.e., it will evaluate to TRUE. This is an optional argument.

For example, if you were to input the formula below into your Excel spreadsheet, the returned result would be 'Good", provided the value inserted in the cell A1 is more than 10:

=IF(A1>10, "Good")

The expression, value_if_false will return the value when the test condition doesn't get met, i.e., it will evaluate to FALSE. This is also an optional argument.

For example, if you input the formula below into your spreadsheet, the returned result would be "Good" provided the value in the cell A1 is more than 10 but, if it is less than 10, the returned result will be "Bad":

=IF(A1>10, "Good", "Bad")

Although everything bar the first argument is optional, if you don't understand what goes on behind the scenes in the IF function then you may not get the result that you want.

Omitting value_if_true

If you leave the value_if_true argument out of your formula, should the condition be met then the returned result will be 0. Here's an example:

=IF(A1>10,, "Bad")

If you do not require a value to be displayed by IF when a condition has been met, you need to add a pair of double quote marks into the second argument, as such:

=IF(A1>10, "", "Bad")

Technically, an empty string would be returned, and the spreadsheet user would not see it. However, it would be visible to other functions, like COUNTA.

Omitting value_if_false

If you are not bothered what happens when a condition doesn't get met, you can leave out the third argument in the IF formula. Should you omit value_if_false and the evaluation of the test is FALSE, you will get the result of FALSE returned. Now, that is not what you would expect to happen here. Have a look at this formula:

=IF(A1>10, "Good")

If you add a comma in following value_if_true, the IF function will then return 0 and this doesn't make a lot of sense either:

=IF(A1>10, "Good,")

The best way to get what you want is to insert the double quote marks as the third argument. The result, should the condition not be met, would be an empty cell:

=IF(A1>10, "Good", "")

How to Make the IF Function Display TRUE or FALSE

If you are looking for the IF formula to show TRUE when a condition is met or FALSE when it isn't, you must type the words in. TRUE must be inserted in the value_if_true argument while FALSE goes in the value_if_false argument. Alternatively, you can leave the value_if_false argument out. Here's an example:

=IF(A1>10, TRUE, FALSE)

or

=IF(A1>10, TRUE)

NOTE – Do not enclose the IF formula in double quotes if you want the Boolean values of TRUE or FALSE to be recognized by other formulas. You should only add the quote marks if you want the values returned as text values. None of the other formulas will recognize text as a logical value.

How to Use IF to Get a Result from a Mathematical Operation

You don't need to have a specific value returned; you can use IF to test a condition, carry out a mathematical operation and then return a value and we do this using the arithmetic operators or other functions in the arguments, value_if_true, and value_if_false. Here are a couple of examples:

=IF(B1>C1, D3*10, D3*5)

This formula is looking at the values in B1 and C1 and is comparing them. Should B1 be greater than C1, the value that is in cell D3 is multiplied by 10; if it not greater, D3 is multiplied by 5.

=IF(B1<>C1, SUM(B1:D1), "")

This formula is looking at the values in B1 and C1 as well and is also comparing them. Should B1 not be equal to C1, the result returned will be the values in cells B1 to D1 summed. If they are equal, then an empty string will be returned.

Operators

Quite a few formulas, especially simple ones, require you to use operators, symbols that indicate what computation is going to be done. There are four types of operator in Excel:

- Arithmetic
- Comparison
- Text
- Reference

Type	Character	Operation	Example
Arithmetic	plus sign (+)	Addition	=A1+B2
	minus sign (-)	Subtraction/negation	=A4-B1 or -D3
	asterisk (*)	Multiplication	=A1*B2
	/	Division	=A1/B2
	%	Percent (division by 100)	=A4%
	^	Exponentiation	=A1^4
Comparison	=	Equal to	=A1=B2
	>	Greater than	=A3>B2
	<	Less than	=A3<B2
	>=	Greater than/Equal to	=A3>=B4
	<=	Less than/Equal to	=B4<=A3
	<>	Not equal to	=A1<>B2

Text	&	Concatenate	=A1&" "&B4
Reference	colon (:)	Range	=SUM(D4:E27)
	comma (,)	Union	
	=SUM(A1,B4:D23,B5)		
	space	Intersection	=SUM(B3:B6 B3:D6)

Mostly, you will use arithmetic operators for your formulas that do not need a function. This is because the arithmetic operators carry out the operation between the values in the specified cells and produce their own mathematical result.

Comparison operators will only produce a Boolean result of TRUE or FALSE, depending on the comparison being made.

The only text operator is the ampersand (&), which is used for joining text entries together.

If you need to include different operator types in your formula, Excel will follow an order of precedence. Should the operators share the same precedence level, they are evaluated on a strict left-to-right basis.

Here is the order of precedence:

Precedence	Operator	Function
1	-	Negation/Subtraction
2	%	Percent
3	^	Exponentiation
4	* and /	Multiplication and Division
5	+ and -	Addition and Subtraction
6	&	Concatenation
7	=,<, >, <=, >=, <>	Comparison operators

Logical Functions

This is an overview of the four logical functions used in Excel for working with logical values. Those functions are:

- AND
- OR
- XOR
- NOT

These four functions can be used when you want to do two or more comparisons in a formula or when you want to test several conditions. Like the logical operators, a logical function will return one of two values – TRUE or FALSE.

Have a look at what each of the functions does so that you know which one to use in any given formula:

- AND - will return TRUE provided all arguments are evaluated as TRUE.
For example, =AND(A1>=10, B3<5). In this formula, we can expect TRUE to be returned if the value in A1 is the same as or greater than 10, AND B3 is less than 5. If not, FALSE is returned.

- OR – will return TRUE provided any of the arguments evaluates as TRUE.
For example, =OR(A1>=10, B3<5). In this formula, we can expect TRU to be returned if A1 is more than 10 OR B3 is less than 5 OR both of these conditions are met. If neither condition is met, FALSE is returned.

- XOR – will return an Exclusive OR of all the arguments. For example, =XOR(A1>=10, B3<5). In this formula, we can expect TRUE to be returned if either A1 is more than or equal to 10 OR B3 is less than 5. If both or none of the conditions are met, FALSE will be returned.
- NOT – will return a reverse of the value of the argument. For example, if the argument evaluated to TRUE, FALSE would be returned, and vice versa. For example, =NOT(A1>=10). In this formula, if the value in A1 is

more than or the same as 10, FALSE will be returned; if otherwise, then TRUE is returned.

When you use logical functions, you may use Boolean values, cell references, text values, numeric values, comparison operators and other functions in the arguments. However, each argument must evaluate to TRUE or FALSE or they must produce arrays or references that have logical values in them.

If there are any empty cells in any argument, these values are ignored. If all arguments are only empty cells, the returned value will be an error - #VALUE!

Should an argument contain a number, zero will be evaluated as FALSE and any non-zero numbers as TRUE, and that includes a negative number. For example, if the cells B2:B25 have numbers in them, the formula =AND(B2:B25) will be returned as TRUE, provided there are no zeros in the cells; if there are, FALSE will be returned.

If the arguments do not evaluate to a logical value, the logical function will return an error of #VALUE!.

An error of #NAME? is returned if the name of the function has not been spelled correctly or you have tried to use a function in a version of Excel that has no support for it. For example, you cannot use XOR in any version of Excel other than 2013 and 2016.

A maximum of 255 arguments may be included in any logical function used in Excel 2007, 2010, 2013 and 2016. The only limit is that the formula length must not be more than 8,192 characters in total. In earlier versions of Excel, the maximum number of arguments is 30 and the formula length must not be more than 1,024 characters.

Next, we are going to look at these in a little more detail.

AND

This is the more popular logical function and is used when you need to test multiple conditions that must all be met. The AND function will test every condition specified and, provided all evaluate TRUE, TRUE will be returned; if not then FALSE is returned.

The syntax is

=AND(logical1, [logical2], ...)

The first condition, logical1, is required and must evaluate to TRUE or FALSE. The rest of the conditions are all optional but, should they be used, they must also evaluate to TRUE or FALSE.

Now, a couple of examples:

=AND(A1="Apples", B1>C1)

In this, we can expect TRUE to be returned if A1 contains "Apples" AND B1 is more than or the same as C1. If not, FALSE is returned

=AND(B1>25, B1=C1)

In this, we can expect TRUE to be returned if B1 is more than 25 AND B1 is equal to C1. If not, FALSE is returned

=AND(A1="Apples", B1>=35, B1>C1)

In this, we can expect TRUE to be returned if A1 contains "Apples," B1 is greater than 35 or equal to it, AND B1 is greater than C1. IF not, FALSE is returned

Common Uses

On its own, the AND function is not the most exciting and it doesn't really have many uses but, combine it with other functions and it can provide a serious boost to your worksheets.

The AND function works best with the IF function, in the logical_test argument because it allows you to test multiple conditions. For example, you can put any AND function in the IF function, known as nesting, and get something like this:

=IF(AND(A1="Apples", B1>C1), "Good", "Bad")

Using the BETWEEN Condition

If you wanted a formula that would get all the values between two specified values, the best way is with the AND function in the logical test of the IF function. Let's say that you have three columns, A, B, and C and each column has one value. You need to know if the value in column A is between the values in B and C. For this formula, all you need is an IF function with the AND function nested in it and some comparison operators:

This first example is checking to see if value 1 is between the values 2 and 3, inclusive:

=IF(AND(A1>=B1,A1<=C1),"Yes", "No")

And this is checking the same but not inclusive:

=IF(AND(A1>B1, A1<C1),"Yes", "No")

This formula will work with all types of data, whether they are numbers, text values or dates. When used for text value comparisons, the formula will check them, in alphabetical order, one character at a time. For example, let's say that your values are:

- Apples
- Apricots
- Bananas

The result from using this formula would be that Apples cannot be in between Apricots and Bananas because the second instance of 'p' in the word Apples is before the 'r' that is in Apricots.

The IF/AND formula is one of the simplest and fastest, not to mention the most versatile and can be used for just about anything in Excel.

OR

OR is another of the common logical functions used for comparison of statements or values. The difference between AND and OR is that the latter will return TRUE if one or more of the arguments are TRUE and FALSE is every argument evaluates to FALSE. The syntax is much the same as the AND function:

=OR(logical1, [logical2], ...)

The first argument is required, the rest are optional. Let's have a look at some formulas so you can see how the OR function gets to work:

=OR(A1="Apples", A1="Lemons")

In this, we can expect TRUE to be returned if A1 has Apples or Lemons in it; if not, FALSE will be returned

=OR(B1>=45, C1>=25)

In this one, we should see TRUE returned if B1 is more than or the same as 45 OR C1 is more then or the same as 25. If not, FALSE will be returned

=OR(B1=" ", C1="")

We can expect TRUE to be returned if either or both of B1 and C1 are blank. IF not, FALSE will be returned.

Just like the AND function OR is also used to make other functions more useful specifically those that are used for logical testing, such as the IF function. Have a look at these examples:

IF with OR

=IF(OR(B1>35, C1>25), "Good", "Bad")

We can expect to see 'Good" returned if the value of B1 is more than 35 OR the value of C1 is more than 25. If not, "Bad" is returned.

AND/OR

There is nothing stopping you from using both the AND function and the OR function in one formula. There are many variations of the basic formulae below:

- =AND(OR(Condition1, Condition2), Condition3)
- =AND(OR(Condition1, Condition2), OR(Condition3, Condition4)
- =OR(AND(Condition1, Condition2), Condition3)
- =OR(AND(Condition1,Condition2), AND(Condition3,Condition4))

Let's be a bit more specific; you want to know how many consignments of apples and lemons have sold out. For this, you want the number in column B, "In Stock," to be the same as the number in column C, "Sold." To find that out, you could use this AND/OR formula:

=OR(AND(A1="apples", B1=C1), AND(A1="lemons", B1=C1))

XOR

The XOR function didn't come into Excel until the 2013 version. XOR is an Exclusive OR function, something that will be familiar to those who know some programming language. If you are not familiar with it, bear with me and you should understand it very shortly. First, the syntax is the same as OR:

=XOR(logical1, [logical2],...)

The first argument is a requirement, the rest are optional. One formula may be used to test up to 254 arguments or conditions and these may be arrays, logical values or references – the only condition is that they must evaluate to TRUE or to FALSE.

The most basic XOR statement would have two logical statements. TRUE will be returned if one of the statements evaluates TRUE. If both or neither of them evaluates TRUE, then FALSE is returned. Let's look at a couple of examples to help you along:

=XOR(2>1, 3<2)   TRUE

TRUE is returned because argument 1 evaluates TRUE and argument 2 evaluates FALSE

=XOR(2<1, 3<2)   FALSE

FALSE is returned because both arguments evaluate to FALSE

=XOR(2>1, 3>2)   FALSE

FALSE is returned because both arguments evaluate to TRUE

That is with two arguments. If you wanted to add more arguments in, you would expect to see:

TRUE returned if an odd number, i.e., 3 or 5, of the arguments are TRUE

FALSE returned if the number of TRUE statements is an even number, i.e., 4 or 6, OR all the statements evaluate FALSE

Let's look at how this function can be used for a real-world scenario. We'll assume that you have a table that has been populated with contestants and the results each has from two games. You want to see which players will be playing game three based on these specific conditions:

Those who won the first and second games will automatically go on to the next round and don't need to play the third game.

Those who lost games one and two will be automatically knocked out and will not play the third game

Those who won the first or the second games will go on to play the third to see who will advance to the next round and who gets knocked out.

We can find all this out with one XOR formula:

=XOR(A2="Won", B2="Won")

And, if you were to nest the XOR function inside the IF formula logical test, the results would make even more sense:

=IF(XOR(A2="Won", B2="Won"), "Yes", "No")

NOT

This must be one of the easiest and simplest of all Excel functions, at least as far as the syntax goes:

=NOT(logical)

We use this function to reverse the value of the argument used with it. In simpler terms, if the argument evaluates to TRUE, then NOT will return a value of FALSE and vice versa. Have a look at these two formulas, both returning a value of FALSE:

=NOT(TRUE)

=NOT(4*4=16)

So, why could you possibly want stupid results like this? Sometimes you might want to know when a specific condition hasn't been met, rather than when it has. For example, when looking a list of clothes, you might want to exclude a specific color that perhaps isn't right for you:

=NOT(C3="yellow")

As you would, by now, expect, there are always multiple ways to achieve something in Excel and you can get the same result as you get with the above formula when you use the operator, NOT equal to:

=C3<>"yellow"

You can also test multiple conditions by using the NOT function together with the AND function and the OR function. For example, we want to leave out yellow and red from the list of colors, so you would do something like this:

=NOT(OR(C3="yellow", C2="red"))

And, if you really don't want a yellow jacket, but you might consider a blue coat or a white t-shirt, you use NOT with AND:

=NOT(AND(C3="yellow", D2="jacket"))

Another use for NOT is to reverse how another function behaves. For example, you could use NOT together with ISBLANK to make ISNOTBLANK – this is one of the formulas that is not included with Excel at the time of writing.

The formula, =ISBLANK(A1) will return TRUE provided A1 is blank. If you added the NOT function in, this result would then be FALSE - =NOT(ISBLANK(A1))

You can go further with this by adding a nested IF to the NOT and ISBLANK functions:

=IF(NOT(ISBLANK(C1)), C1*0.25, "No bonus :(")

What this formula is doing is telling Excel that if the cell C1 is not completely empty, the value in it should be multiplied by 0.25. This provides a 25% bonus for all who made more sales but if C1 is blank then "No bonus" is the result.

LEN

LEN is one of the most straightforward of all Excel functions and it stands for 'length.' The function is used to return the length of a cell or of a text string. This includes all spaces, special character, letters, and numbers. It only has a single argument:

=LEN(text)

Text is where you want to count the characters in a text string; if you wanted numbers, you would change that; Have a look at these example formulas:

=LEN(123)

This will return 3 because there are three numbers in the argument.

=LEN("great")

This will return 5 because the word "great" has got five letters in it. As with other functions, the text strings must be inside a set of double quote marks – these are not counted by LEN.

When you do your own formulas, you will more than likely be using cell references and not text strings or numbers to count the number of characters in a cell range or in a single cell. For example, if you wanted to get the length of a text string in cell B1, you would do this:

=LEN(B1)

When you first look at the LEN function it looks so simplistic that you don't really need any more information about it. But, there are a few things that you can do with LEN to make your formulas do what you want.

Counting Characters in a Single Cell

You already know that LEN will count everything in a specified cell or range and that includes spaces, be they trailing, leading or in between words. Look at this example:

=LEN("Life is Beautiful 2")

The returned result would be 19 – 15 letters, a number, and 3 spaces.

Counting Characters in a Range of Cells

If you wanted to count the characters from several cells individually, include the cell in your formula and then copy it to several more cells, perhaps using the fill handle and dragging it to encompass the cells you want to be included. Once the formula has been copied, LEN will return the number of characters for each individual cell.

Again, bear in mind that LEN will count everything, including all punctuation, quotes, numbers, letters, and spaces.

If you wanted to add up the characters in several cells and get the total, you could do it in two ways:

Add several LEN functions together:

=LEN(B1)+LEN(B2)+LEN(B3)

Alternatively, you can use SUM to add up the characters that LEN returns:

=SUM(LEN(B1),LEN(B2),LEN(B3))

Whichever way you choose, the result will be the total length of all the characters in the specified cells.

CONCATENATE

One thing you will find is that the data in your worksheets may not always be structured how you need it to be. Sometimes you might need to take the content from on cell and split it over multiple cells or you might want to combine all the data from multiple columns into just one column. All this required a function called CONCATENATION. Most commonly, this is used for joining names with addresses, dates with times, text with a value from another formula, and so on.

CONCATENATE is a useful function and there are two ways to use it to join data in your spreadsheets – merging cells or concatenating the values of several cells. Merging cells means that you are merging the contents of at least two cells into just one, giving you one large cell that covers multiple columns and/or rows.

Concatenating cells, on the other hand, means that you are only combining the values of the cells – joining them together. We often use this for combining text from multiple cells (technically, text strings) or adding a value from a formula into a text string.

The syntax of the CONCATENATE function is:

=CONCATENATE(text1, [text2], ...)

Text is the string, value or cell reference and, as with all other functions, only the first argument is required; the rest are optional. Let's look at a few examples of how to use CONCATENATE:

- **Concatenate the values from multiple cells**
The easiest formula, if you want to combine the values from cells B2 and C2 is:

=CONCATENATE(B2, C2)

The result will be shown as the two values together without a delimiter, such as a comma or a space. If you want the values to be separated by a space, you would need to input the double quote marks as argument 2, like this:

=CONCATENATE(B2, " ", C2)

- **Concatenate a text string with a cell value**

You are not limited to using CONCATENATE for joining values together; you can use it for combining text strings so that you get a much better result:

=CONCATENATE(B2, " ", C2, "finished")

This formula tells you that a specific project has been finished – note that a space has been added to the beginning of the world " finished" – this is so that the concatenated strings are separated.

Text strings can be added to the start, middle or end of a CONCATENATE formula:

=CONCATENATE("Look ", B2, " ", C2)

Again, we added a space, indicated by the double quote marks, between the values that we want to combine. That way, there will be a space between the two concatenated strings.

- **Concatenate a text string and a value from another formula**

If you want the returned result from a formula to be better understood, you can use CONCATENATE to combine it with a text string that tells us what that value is. For example, if you wanted to return the date today, you would do this:

=CONCATENATE("Today is ",TEXT(TODAY(), "dd-mm-yy"))

Things to Note

To make sure that you always get the result you want from the CONCATENATE function, follow these rules:

- There must be a minimum of one "text" argument for the function to work
- Each CONCATENATE formula can take up to 255 strings or a maximum of 8,192 characters
- A CONCATENATE function will always return a text string as the result, regardless of whether numbers are used as the source values
- The CONCATENATE function will not recognize an array. You must list each cell reference separately, for example, you would input =CONCATENATE(B1, B2, B3) and not =CONCATENATE(B1:B3)
- If one or more of the arguments in the CONCATENATION formula is invalid, the result will be a #VALUE! error.

Using the & Operator

The & operator, or 'ampersand,' is often used for concatenating cells. This is a very useful method because it is far easier and quicker to type "&" than it is to keep typing "CONCATENATE." This operator can be used for combining cell values, returned results from another function and text strings.

Let's look at some examples of the CONCATENATION operator being used. We are going to redo the formulas we wrote above:

Concatenating the values in B2 and C2:

=B2&C2

Concatenating the values in B2 and C2 with a space:

=B2&" "&C2

Concatenating the values from B2 and C2 with a text string:

=B2 & C2 & " finished"

Concatenating a string with the result of TEXT/TODAY:

="Today is " & TEXT(TODAY(), "dd-mmm-yy")

So, given that both CONCATENATE and the & operator both provide the exact same results, which way is best?

In essence, there is only one real difference between the CONCATENATE function and the & operator and that is the limit of 255 strings maximum in CONCATENATE and the fact that the & operator has no such limit – you can add together as many strings as you want. Besides that, both are identical in what they do and the speed at which they do it, so it comes down to personal preference.

And, to be fair, the limit of 255 strings is a large number and it will be a very rare occurrence that we actually need to concatenate any more than that. Some of you will find it far easier to start off with CONCATENATE, as it may be easier to read, moving on to & as you get more experienced.

Using Special Characters with CONCATENATE

Sometimes you may need to use other characters to join your values together, such as commas, apostrophes, spaces, any other punctuation character, a slash or a hyphen, for example. This is very easy to do; all you do is add the character that you want to use into your formula. You know how to add a space; adding another character is the same, but you must ensure that the character is enclosed in the double quotes, as you can see from these examples:

Concatenating two cells using a space:

=CONCATENATE(B2, " ", C2)

OR

=B2 & " " & C2

Concatenating two cells using a comma:

=CONCATENATE(B2, ", ", C2)

OR

=B2 & ", " & C2

Concatenating two cells using a hyphen:

=CONCATENATE(B2, "-", C2)

OR

=B2 & "-" & C2

TRIM

Sometimes, you may want to compare two or more columns for duplicate entries that you know are in there but the formula you are using just can't locate even one duplicate entry. Maybe you are trying to add together the values from two columns, but the result is consistently just zeros. And why do you keep getting N/A from your VLOOKUP formulas when you know that they are correct. These are just some of the problems that you may come across, all of which are caused by one thing – extra spaces in your text and numeric values in the cells. These spaces may be at the beginning, the end or somewhere in the middle of your values and there is one easy way to remove them – the TRIM function.

The TRIM function can be used for removing extraneous spaces, deleting any leading or trailing spaces or those tucked in the middle. The only ones it will not delete are the single spaces that separate each word. The syntax is dead simple:

=TRIM(text)

Text is the cell that you want to be cleaned up. For example, if you wanted to get rid of the extra spaces in cell B2, you would do this:

=TRIM(B2)

It really is that easy,

Should your data also have non-printing characters or line breaks, the TRIM function can be used together with the CLEAN function to get rid of the first 32 of the non-printing characters present in the ASCII (7-bit) code system.

For example, if you wanted to remove all the line breaks, spaces and any other characters that you don't want from cell B2, you would use this:

=TRIM(CLEAN(B2))

Let's look at some examples of using TRIM, some specific uses and some of the pitfalls that you may fall foul of, as well as the solutions.

Trimming spaces from a column - text

Let's say that you have a whole column full of names. These names have a bit of whitespace at the beginning and the end and extra spaces added in between each word. How do we get rid of all this extra space, all at the same time? Simple – we copy one TRIM formula across the entire column and replace the formula with the correct values. Follow these steps:

We want a TRIM function for the first cell in the column, B2:

=TRIM(B2)

Place your mouse cursor at the bottom right corner of the cell with the formula in it and, when the mouse cursor becomes a +, double-click to copy it down the whole column, up to the last cell that contains data. The result will be two columns – the original one and the new one with all the spaces trimmed out.

Lastly, take the trimmed data and replace the original values with it. Do be careful here – you do not want to copy the trimmed column to the original column as your formulas would be wiped out. You only need to copy the values, none of the formulas, like this:

Using your mouse, select the cells that contain the TRIM formula

Now press CTRL+C so that they are copied

Now do the same to select the cells that contain the original data and then press on CTRL+ALT+V. Then press V again. This is the Paste Special shortcut that will paste the values only

Press the Enter key and you're done.

Removing Leading Spaces from a column - numeric

As you saw, we used the TRIM function to get rid of the extra spaces from a text column without any trouble at all. But, what if your column contains numbers and not text? You could use the same formula as above:

=TRIM(B2)

You might think, on first look, that the function has been successful but look a little closer and you will see that something is wrong – the values that we trimmed are not behaving as numbers. These are some of the indicators that something isn't right:

The original column of data that has the leading spaces and the column that has the trimmed numbers in it are both aligned to the left, regardless of whether you format the numbers or not. Proper numbers are aligned, by default, to the right.

When you select at least two cells that contain trimmed numbers, the status bar on your worksheet will show COUNT. When you are dealing with numbers, you should also see AVERAGE and SUM

When you apply a SUM function to the cells you trimmed, the result will be zero.

So, using the TRIM function here hasn't worked because it hasn't removed the spaces properly. By all accounts, the values you trimmed are text strings – was wanted numbers. This is easy enough to fix – simply multiply all the values you trimmed by 1. Perhaps a better way would be to insert TRIM into the VALUE function, like this:

=VALUE(TRIM(B2))

This formula will remove the leading spaces and the trailing spaces if there are any, and the value that results will be turned into a number.

Removing Leading Spaces Only – Left TRIM

Sometimes you may input duplicate or triplicate spaces in between words, just to make your data look and read better. However, we want to get rid of the leading spaces. Using the TRIM function will remove all spaces, including those extra ones you deliberately inserted and want to keep. To remove the leading space but leave the in=between spaces, the formula is a little bit more complex:

=MID(B2,FIND(MID(TRIM(B2),1,1),B2),LEN(B2))

In this formula, we have used a combination of functions:

- FIND
- MID
- TRIM

Together, these functions work to find the position of the first character (text) in the string. That positional number is then passed to the second MID function which will return the whole string, the length of which has been calculated using LEN. The starting position is that of the first character – the leading spaces have been removed.

Lastly, you can follow the steps from earlier to put the trimmed values into the original text.

Counting the Extra Spaces in a Single Cell

On occasion, before you get rid of the extra spaces in a worksheet, you might want to find out how many there are. To do this in a single cell, we use LEN to work out the total length of the string and then we calculate how long the string would be without the spaces and, finally, subtract that number from the first number:

=LEN(B2)-LEN(TRIM(B2))

MIN and MAX

MIN and MAX functions are used for finding the lowest and the highest values respectively in a specified range of cells.

MIN

Used for finding the lowest value in a cell range, the syntax for MIN is:

=MIN(range_of_cells)

For example, to find the lowest value in the range G2:G45, you would type this formula:

=MIN(G2:G45)

MAX

Used for finding the highest value in a cell range, the syntax for MAX is:

=MAX(range_of_cells)

For example, to find the highest value in the range G2:G45, you would use this formula:

=MAX(G2:G45)

Using IF with MIN

We already know that there is a SUMIF function in Excel along with a COUNTIF function, but there isn't one for MINIF. Instead, you need to create your own and you can do that by combining the two functions together in one array formula.

In this example, we will search for the lowest value of a specified product in a list called Sales, containing several products. As we don't have a Sales list, you can either draw one up or just follow this by reading:

First, type into D2:

=MIN(IF(

This combines the MIN and IF functions

Now, you would input the reference to the product name in the list called Sales and lock the reference using F4:

=MIN(IF(F$3:$F$27

Add a (=) equal sign and then click the cell that contains the criteria for the product name. We are not locking this reference:

=MIN(IF($F$3:$F$27=D2

Add a comma and then choose the quantity cells from the Sales list. Again, lock the reference using F4

=MIN(IF($F$3:$F$27=D2,$G$2:$G$17

TO finish off, add a pair of closing brackets and then press the CTRL+SHIFT+ENTER keys on your keyboard to array-enter:

=MIN(IF($F$3:$F$27=D2,$G$2:$G$17))

Using IF with MAX

Like MINIF, there is no MAXIF function in Excel and you need to create your own. Again, you simply combine the MAX function and the IF function in an array and you do it in exactly the same way as you did with MIN, replacing MIN with MAX.

Multiple Criteria and MAXIF

MAXIF can also be used with multiple criteria, simply by adding in as many IF functions as you require. Have a look at the example formula:

=MAX(IF($F$3:$F$27=D4,IF($I$3:$I$27=$D$2,$J$3:$J$27)))

VLOOKUP

Having left the best until nearly last, this is, without a doubt, one of the most useful of all the Excel functions. However, it is also the least understood function and one of the more intricate.

So, what, exactly is VLOOKUP and what does it do? Well, we know that it is an Excel function and, as to what it does, it will search for a specified value and will return a value that matches from a different column. A bit more specifically – you specify a range of cells and VLOOKUP will look for a value in column one and return a value from another column that is in the same row.

The 'V' in VLOOKUP means 'vertical' and it is the only thing that differentiates itself from HLOOKUP, which I will cover briefly next. For now, the syntax for VLOOKUP is:

=VLOOKUP(lookup_value, table_array, col_index_num, [range_lookup])

There are 4 arguments with this function, the first three are required, the last is an optional one. Let's break that down:

lookup_value – specifies the value you want to find. This may be a number, a date, text, a cell reference with a value, or a value returned by another function. For example:

=VLOOKUP(35, A3:B17, 3)

The number 35 will be searched for

=VLOOKUP("bananas," A1:B17, 3)

The text "bananas" will be searched for – do remember that text values must be inside double quote marks.

=VLOOKUP(C3, A1:B17, 3)

A value in the cell C3 is going to be searched for.

table_array – this specifies at least two data columns. VLOOKUP will search for the lookup_value in the first column specified in table_array. This may have text, numbers, dates or logical values in it. One thing to keep in mind is that values are not case sensitive, so it doesn't matter if you use upper or lowercase. So, our first formula example will search for the number "35" in cells A3 to B17 – A is the initial column in table_array. Make sense?

col_index_num - this specifies the number of the column in table_array from where the value in the row that corresponds to is returned. The columns in the table run from left to right so the left-most one is 1 in the array and so on.

So, let's look at that formula again:

=VLOOKUP(35, A3:B17, 3)

Using the required parameters, we now know that the formula will look for "35" in cells A3 to B17 and will return the value that matches from column B (the second column in the table).

range_lookup – this is the optional argument and it is used when you want an approximate match (TRUE or left out) or you want an exact match (FALSE).

Now let's look at some examples that show you how to use VLOOKUP on real data.

Using VLOOKUP from a Different Worksheet

Most of the time, VLOOKUP is not used for finding values in the same worksheet; usually, it is for finding data in a different one. To do this, you need to specify the name of the worksheet followed by an exclamation mark inside table_array and must be inserted before you include the cell range. For example:

=VLOOKUP(35, Sheet4!A3:B17,3)

This formula is telling VLOOKUP that it needs to look in cell range A3:B17 in Sheet4.

In the next example, VLOOKUP will look for a text of "Product 4" in the B column of the worksheet called "Prices."

=VLOOKUP("Product 4",Prices!$B$2:$C$9,2,FALSE)

Using VLOOKUP from a Different Workbook

In this formula, as well as specifying the sheet name, you must specify the name of the workbook inside square brackets []. Have a look at the following example:

=VLOOKUP(35,[Numbers.xlsx]Sheet4!A3:B17, 3)

This formula is looking for value "35" in Sheet4 of the workbook named "Numbers.xlsx".

If there are any spaces or any characters that are not alphabetical in the name of the workbook or the worksheet, they must be placed inside a set of single quote marks, like this:

=VLOOKUP(35,'[Numbers.xlsx]Sheet4'!A3:B17,3)

Using a Named Range or Table

If you need to use the same range in multiple VLOOKUP formulas, the easiest way is to make a named range and then, when you need to use it, you can just type the name of the range into table_array. To do this, simply highlight the cells that you want in your range and, in the Name box on the left side of the formula bar, type in the name you are giving it. Now, to get the price of Product 4, from the earlier example, you could just type this:

=VLOOKUP("Product 4",Products,3)

Normally, a range name will apply to a whole workbook so there is no need to add the name of the worksheet. However, if you are looking in a different workbook, you still need to add the name of the workbook before the range:

=VLOOKUP("Product 4",PriceList.xlsx!Products,3)

The Wildcard Character

The wildcard character can be used in many different formulas, including VLOOKUP and these are the ones you can use:

- ? – the question mark. This will match one character
- - the asterisk. This will match a character sequence

Using these characters can prove useful sometimes, for example:

- When you forget the exact text you want to search for
- If you wanted to search for a word that is only part of the contents of the cell
- When there are trailing or leading spaces in a lookup column

Now for some examples:

- **Looking for text that starts or ends with a specific character:**

Let's say that you want to find a specific name in a database. You have forgotten the surname, but you remember that it back with "bil." So, you would use this VLOOKUP formula:

=VLOOKUP("bil",$B$3:$D$17,2,FALSE)*

When you are certain you have located the right name, you can them use another VLOOKUP formula that is similar, to find out how much the customer paid. To do that, change parameter 3 to the correct column number, in our case, it is column D:

=VLOOKUP("bil",$B$3:$D$17,2,FALSE)*

Here are some more VLOOKUP examples using wildcard characters:

=VLOOKUP("*lam",$B$3:$D$18,2,FALSE)

This formula will look for a name that ends with "lam".

=VLOOKUP("co*ath",$B$3:$D$18,2,FALSE)

This formula will look for the name that begins with "co" and ends with "ath".

=VLOOKUP("??????",$B$3:$D$18,2,FALSE)

This formula will look for a surname with 6 characters in it.

NOTE – When you use a wildcard character, you must always put FALSE in for the last argument. Should the lookup range have more than one matching entry, the returned value will be the first one.

Things to Remember

- VLOOKUP will always look for a lookup value in the column of table_array that is furthest to the left
- VLOOKUP values are not case-sensitive
- If lookup_value is less than the smallest value specified in table_array, column 1, an #N/A error is returned
- If argument 3 – col_index_num – is lower than 1, the #VALUE error is returned. If it is more than the total number of table_array columns, the #REF error is returned.

HLOOKUP

HLOOKUP is much the same as VLOOKUP but with one difference – the H stands for Horizontal and the function is used for looking up and retrieving data from specified rows. The syntax is also similar to VLOOKUP:

=HLOOKUP (value, table, row_index, [range_lookup])

The first three arguments are required while the fourth is optional. Let's look into the formula:

value - the value that you want to find

table – the table you want the data retrieved from

row_index – the number of the row where the data is to be retrieved from

range_lookup - optional

So, how does it work? HLOOKUP will search the first row of a specified table to find a specified value. The difference between HLOOKUP and VLOOKUP is:

- HLOOKUP is for finding values in the first row of a specified table
- VLOOKUP is for finding values in the first column of a specified table

Range_lookup, the optional argument, is for when you might want an exact match to a value. The default for this argument is TRUE, which allows for an approximate match while FALSE will find an exact match.

Example Formula

Take this example of an HLOOKUP formula:

=HLOOKUP("",range,1,FALSE)*

If you wanted to find the first value (text) across a specified range of column you would use a wildcard character, such as the asterisk.

Let's throw some actual values and references in so you can see it better:

=HLOOKUP("*",D6:F6,1,0)

The value for the lookup is an asterisk (*), a wildcard character that will match with at least one text value.

D6:F6 is the table array

The row is number 1 because there is only one row in our range

O is the range argument. This indicates FALSE which will force HLOOKUP to find an exact match to the value.

HLOOKUP will find the first value (text) in columns D through F in each of the rows

Empty Strings

Sometimes, other formulae will produce empty strings, but you don't want to bother these. To ignore them, you simply adjust your wildcards:

=HLOOKUP("?*",range,1,0)

In this, HLOOKUP will match the text with one or more characters.

NOTE – This only works for text values, not numeric, because the asterisk wildcard only matches text.

Formula How-To's

Now that you have some idea of basic formulas in Excel, use these tips to guide you on using them effectively and not falling foul of common errors:

Do not re-type one formula into several cells; copy it

There is no need to type the same formula into multiple adjacent cells. Use the fill handle in the bottom corner of the highlighted cell and drag it down or across the cells. If you want an entire column filled with the same formula in each cell, double-click your mouse on the plus sign on the fill handle.

NOTE – do check that the references are correct – depending on if they are relative or absolute references, they may have changed.

Delete a Formula Without Deleting the Calculated Value

When you delete a formula using the Del key on your keyboard, the calculated value will also be removed. You can delete just the formula and retain the calculated value:

- Highlight all the cells with the formulas you want to be deleted
- Press on CTRL+C to copy them
- Right-click your mouse and then choose Paste Values>Values from the drop-down menu. This will paste the values into the cells while removing the formula.

Text Values Should Be IN Double Quote Marks

But number values shouldn't. Any text value that is in a formula must be inside a set of double quotation marks ("") but, if you do the same to a number value, Excel will see it as text and treat it as such. For example, if you wanted to check a value in cell B3 and then return the number 1 for "Passed" or 0 if not, you would input this formula into C3:

=IF(C2="pass", 1, 0)

Now copy that formula down to the other cells and you will see you have a column full of 0's and 1's that you can easily calculate.

Now try it with double quotes around the numbers:

=IF(C2="pass", "1", "0")

To start with, the output looks as it should, a column of 0's and 1's but look a little closer and you will spot that the values have been left-aligned in the cells. This means they are text strings and not the numbers you want. Later, if you were to try calculating them, you would end up wondering why a COUNT or SUM formula that is perfectly correct will only return 0.

Never Format Numbers

This is a very easy rule to remember and it is very important. You should never enter any formatted number into your formulas, formatting such as the dollar sign or a comma, for example.

The dollar sign ($) is used to make a cell reference absolute while the comma is the default used for separating arguments. If you were to format your numbers using those characters, Excel will not be happy. Instead of typing in $1,500, just type 1500 – you can format the output however you want.

Make Sure Opening and Closing Parentheses Match

This is one of the biggest mistakes rookies make. Whenever you craft a complicated formula, one that has several nested functions in it, you will be using multiple sets of parentheses to tell Excel the order of the calculations. Do make sure that your parentheses are paired properly – for every opening parenthesis, there must be a closing one. To make life a little easier for you, when you enter a formula like this or edit one, Excel will show each set of parentheses in different colors – finding the matches should be much easier.

Troubleshooting Tips for Formulas and Functions

Sometimes it can seem as if nothing is going right in your spreadsheet. Errors are all part and parcel of Excel, but most of the time they are very easy to fix. Here are some of the best troubleshooting tips to help you:

Error values are not a pain

When Excel is unable to calculate your formula, it will throw up an error message. Rather than seeing these as a pain, use them as a clue to spot where you went wrong These are the most common error values you will see:

- **#DIV/0** – your formula has a reference to a cell that either evaluates to or contains 0 or has nothing in it – Excel is not able to divide by zero.
- **#NAME?** – you have incorrectly referenced a range, or you did not put text inside the double quote marks. Excel tries to interpret text as a range name, a cell reference or the name of a function. If it doesn't recognize the text as being one of these, you will see this error. Check your names, check that you have used a name that exists, look at your cell references and lastly, make sure you have used the double quotes.
- **#NULL!** – you have referenced an intersection between ranges that cannot intersect, like B1:D4 or F5:H7. If the ranges can intersect, then you may have used a space and not a comma to separate the range references.
- **#NUM!** – there is an issue with a number in your formula – the argument may be invalid, or the result is too small or too large
- **#REF!** – a cell has not been referenced properly. More than likely, one has been deleted
- **#VALUE!** – an incorrect operator or data type has been used

Evaluate Individual Components

The quickest way to find a problem is to go through each component, one at a time. You can do this in the cell itself or you can use the formula bar. Highlight the cell and press on F9. Excel will now evaluate the reference and will return the result in the Formula bar. If you want to edit in the cell, double-click on the cell.

Look for Multiple Lines

If your formula looks a bit too simple, highlight it and look at the Formula bar – the right end of it to be specific. If you see a double arrow, it indicates that you have got multiple lines in the formula. Click on the downward arrow to go through each line or click on Expand Formula Bar and the entire formula will be displayed. To separate each component of the formula, put the cursor where you want a new line and press the ALT+ENTER keys. If you break the expressions down across multiple lines, it can be easier to see the logic in the expression.

Easily Check Formulas by Displaying Them

To display all your formulas, press CTRL+~ (the tilde sign is to the left of the number 1 on your keyboard's top number bar. Press it again, and it will toggle the results. This will display your formulas, so you can check them all for consistency and any errors. You can, if you want, print these all off so you can edit them without staring at your screen for too long.

Select Your Formula Cells

If you have a large and complex worksheet, finding all your formula cells can be somewhat tedious and time-consuming. You are liable to miss a few, especially if your memory and/or eyesight are not quite what they used to be! Excel can take the hard work out of this and here's how:

- Press the F5 key and the Go To dialog box will appear.
- At the bottom of the dialog box is a Special button – click this
- A window will now load, check the option for Formulas
- Click on OK and you will be shown all the formulas in your sheet
- From here, you can scan through them or do whatever you want to them

Is It A Date? Is It A Number? No, It's an Error!

On occasion, one of your formulas may return a time or a date value when all you wanted was a number. This normally happens when your formula is referencing a cell that you formatted as time or date. This means that your formula is correct; all you need to do is change the referenced cell to the correct one and the error value will go

Be Aware of Character Limits

Before Excel 2007, formulas were limited to being no more than 1,024 characters long. After Excel 2007, that was changed to 8,192. It is highly unlikely that you will ever need to use that many characters though! It is also worth noting that Excel 2010 onwards can take up to 255 arguments per formula and up to 64 nested functions.

Your Function Has Returned a Function!

If you have input a function and pressed ENTER as you should, and Excel merely displays your function, then it is seeing the contents of the cell as text. You can fix this in one of two ways:

- If you have added an apostrophe to the start of the function by mistake, simply delete it
- Ensure that you didn't format as Text. If you did, you need to change it to something better, perhaps General

Your Formula Will Not Recalculate

Your formula is correct, you know the function works and it was all just fine until you went in and changed an independent value. Now your function won't recalculate and give you an updated result. The best possible reason for this is that you managed to turn Automatic Recalculations off. It's easy to do this while you are working away and either not realize or forget to put it back on again but resetting it is very easy:

- Click on File and then on Options. If you are using Excel 2003, click on Tools and then Options and, in Excel 2007, click on the Office button and then on Excel Options
- In the left-hand pane, click on Formulas and then click on Calculations
- Make sure the option for Automatic is checked
- Click on OK

Everything will work just as it should now.

Conclusion

First, I want to thank you for taking the time to read my guide. Although I couldn't possibly cover every single function and the formulas that go with it, I hope that I have been able to give you an idea of the most common ones. These functions are the ones you will use the most when you are getting started in Excel, the functions that will make your life much easier. The rest, the complex ones, will come later when you have the experience in basic Excel spreadsheet usage and are looking to further your knowledge.

For now, practice these, learn every variation, how they all work, what they do. Play around with them, run different formulas - you have an idea of how to write these formulas now – and see what results you get. And, when you are ready, move on to the next stage, the more complex functions, and formulas.

Excel is an incredibly useful tool, be it for running your business or for personal use. More than any other program in the Microsoft Office Suite, it is the one you should take the time to learn.

References

https://www.howtogeek.com

https://www.thoughtco.com

http://quadexcel.com/

https://www.ablebits.com

https://www.techrepublic.com

Excel power query

Excel for Beginners

Table of Contents

Chapter 1

Excel Power Query Editor: Excel for Beginners

Introduction:

Microsoft, the tech giant, is known for its new innovation and user-friendly products.

While you would love the new products it has on offer, from the Surface Book to the Surface Studio, the one thing that most people can never forget is just how useful some of the Microsoft software is.

Who doesn't use Microsoft Word for one - even Mac users can't ignore its utility.

Businesses love the Microsoft Excel for its ability to keep records – but as we shall see below, it goes a lot more than just helping you stay up to day.

Microsoft Excel: A Look

Microsoft has now come out with an updated version of Excel 2010. The new version of the Microsoft Excel 2013 proves out to be a lifesaver for the user, who wants loads of information just with one click. The new changing scenario's and the tech savvy world, both will look forward to this new product from Microsoft which is basically made for quick accessibility.

Excel 2013 comes with many additions in terms of tools. The new program comes with the addition of the 'Touch Mode' Option. It also offers co authoring with the help of Sky Drive along with the built in sharing menu. Flash feature introduced in this version of Excel will help the user in many ways. The user can now keep an eye on what he has stored in his spread sheet.

The Quick analysis tool, when selected will expand itself into a selection box. Just by keeping the mouse held on the selected option will give the user a preview of the changes done. The user with the help of this tool can do with the selected data what he wants to do for ex- formatting, tables, spark lines, etc. The new version of Excel 2013 will give the user an edge by placing before him such options which will give him enhanced accessibility.

The new version is much better from the previous one in all respects, however collaboration feature needs more refining and innovation to be done by the company.

User accessibility and simultaneous editing are just ready to blast the software market along with the increased focus on the new Cloud technology. Microsoft's new version will score out in the market due to the above said reasons.

Artificial Intelligence and Microsoft Excel

We are living in a time when Artificial Intelligence and Big Data rule the IT world. All the applications are so designed to need minimum human interference. This speeds up the processing time as well as reduces the chances of human errors.

We get a whole range of programs dedicated specifically for automation of various applications. There is a sea of information in the virtual space which needs to be collected, sorted and analyzed. Doing these manually is neither possible nor efficient way of doing so. To perform such tasks, there are a lot of dedicated applications like Hadoop and Azure performing big data analysis.

MS-Excel has always been associated with collection and analysis of data. With ever-developing technology, MS-Excel Power Query was introduced to meet the new-age business demands. It comes with better technology for collecting data from various sources and their analysis for desired information.

Power Query is a free Excel-add-in meant for enhancing self-service business intelligence. It uses data across all big data software like azure marketplace and OData and allows the analysts to make proper manipulations to them for a better analysis. This empowers them to make informed business decisions.

Today, the role of business analysts is mostly dependent upon these analytical tools. This enables them to give calculated advice and also proper risk-management for various projects.

1.1 Data analysis (Business Intelligence)

Having access to right information at the right time gives power to organizations. Easy to use Business Intelligence tools create high value, while helping companies stay ahead of their competitors.

This means that with its help, your organization can stay ahead of the competition by providing you the correction information at the right time with minimal efforts. You don't have to worry about looking for data in multiple places, learning complex SQL statements to find out the business information. You will find it easy to deal with an increasing number of reports, dashboards and natural-language query engines which can be used by business users without any technical support.

In this digital world, every business generates tons of data, that needs to be collected, cleaned, related (to each other), stored in a central place and most importantly, they should be accessible to business users in an easy interface. Converting data to valuable information is a key success factor helping organizations make right decisions.

You must have noticed that you begin to get advertisements on your web browsers which actually are related to your previous web searches. How does that happen? Let us explain that with an example. You searched on Google for best management courses across the country. This information went into the virtual space, and after analysis by various AI and Big data software, it was concluded that you might be interested in a particular college or a course. But, other colleges don't want to lose out.

They also want to attract your attention. Use your IP address is traced by these AI and Big Data software used by the colleges. And, you begin to receive notifications regarding various management colleges. These institutes utilize the technology to attract your attention. This is a very small example of how business intelligence works.

There are scores of applications that efficiently refine out the information from web space and then use them for business purposes. Imagine the scores of business flourishing on the e-space just because of these two technical advancements.

Business intelligence allows the decision makers to make informed decisions. These, in turn, pave the way to better business plans, better execution and ultimately increased revenue.

Often we come across a reputed brand entering a new business. Do they enter on their whims and fancies? No.

Their decision makers and analysts first thoroughly study that particular market. They select the niche for themselves. Let us explain it with an example. There is some company X. If they are venturing into the clothing business, their analysts determine if it would be profitable to be specific for men, women and kids or just for plus sized people. Currently, not many companies manufacture plus sized clothes.

So, company X will have a very few competitors. And, if they analyze the market and fashion trends, the company X is bound to succeed.

This data analysis was not so profound few years back. Most of the nations were closed economy and their domestic market had few players. But with most of the nations becoming open economies, the competition for each and every segment of the market has increased manifold. Just for a small thing like a toothbrush, we have now more than 500 companies including domestic and MNCs.

In such severe competition, a good business analyst needs a backing of an efficient data analytic tool. Power query fills this gap and empowers business analysts to function efficiently.

Business intelligence software ensures all these analytical tasks are accurately conducted, and hence, they are a major factor in success stories. They enable the policy makers to collect the data and refine them to suit their needs.

1.2 Power Query

While analyzing a set of data, one needs to first collect them from various sources. These sources contain data as tables, graphs pie charts etc. One needs to study them carefully and then mould them into another analytical representation. Microsoft Power BI self-service solution introduced power query as an add-in to ease this process.

With its interactive user interface, power query allows to search, detect, refine, associate, convert and modify data as well. A business decision maker needs to gather information from various sources across the internet. Power Query can be easily used for searching such stats..

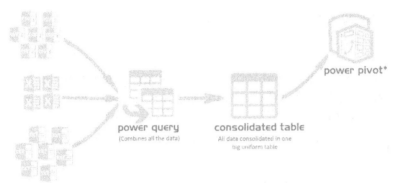

power pivot*

power query
(Combines all the data)

consolidated table
All data consolidated in one
big uniform table

* Optional direct load of the consolidated table to Power Pivot
Note: Power Query can handle all the desired file types at the same time or you can always filter the steps to only handle a certain file type

The best part of Power Query is that it allows importing from any data source. Some of the data sources are:

a. Web sources

b. CSV, XML, Excel, any folder with metadata and links

c. SQL Server, Oracle, IBM DB2, MySQL, Windows Azure SQL Database

d. SharePoint list, Windows Azure Blob Storage, Facebook and so on.

So why is PowerQuery so much in demand?

We need to realize that today's world heavily depends on utilizing each and every second. The business analysts have a very important role in ensuring that their concerned business functions properly. In this vast world, an analysis is always needed.

However, analysts had to work pretty hard, to get something that was not worth their time. Even if they needed to compare two sets of data, they had to spend too much time. Their potential was getting wasted. They had to copy-paste data from one source to the excel sheets.

Then there was the need to manually arrange them, analyze them and derive the result. It was realized that there was a dearth of an automation tool which would especially target the business enterprises. PowerQuery is the brainchild of this demand. By using PowerQuery, the business analysis has become very simple and time efficient.

Those analysts who had to spend two to three hours in just organizing and analyzing data can now do so in a matter of minutes. Their potential can now be fully utilized. Also, the process has become error-proof and fast.

PowerQuery has truly revolutionized the business enterprise.

1.3 Why should you use PowerQuery?

Everyone is going mad over PowerQuery. It is the hottest technology right now. Everyone wants to learn it. But what is so different about it? Why should you invest your time in learning this new software? Isn't it just an extension of MS-Excel?

We have got answers to all your questions. Yes, PowerQuery is actually an add-in of MS-Excel. And, it is totally worth your time. In fact, it will save you a lot of time. If you do any of the following jobs, you should learn this as soon as possible:

a. Collecting data manually from various sources.

b. Creating Excel sheets and feeding data manually

c. Analyzing and interpreting data

d. Cross-checking data to ensure it is error-proof.

e. Reshape data for the correct excel format

f. Write too many Vlookups every day to combine tables.

All these works together with many new functions can be easily performed with just PowerQuery.

Data collection, organization and analysis are completely automated with this. You only need to feed the data sources; rest will be done by the software. In short, you can perform following functions comfortably with the use of Power Query.

a. Discover data across various platforms

b. Find connections between seemingly unrelated data sets

c. Import data sets from various external as well as internal sources.

d. Create custom tables, columns for your data

e. Merge, add, delete or reshape the tables. You can even rename them.

f. Create a new query from two queries

g. Create data visualizations for big data platforms

h. Share queries online and also among your colleagues

This will save you from useless efforts and save you lots of time. Just imagine your efficiency when you will not have to do the lethargic work of manually analyzing the different datasets!

Chapter 2

Getting started with Power Query

Power query may not be present in every Excel version, especially Excel 2010.

Here, we will guide you on how to install it. In Excel 2016, it is known as Get & Transform. PowerQuery is so much efficient that everyone related to an analytical job should learn it. With just basic excel skills, one can perform refined functions with different sets of data quite easily.

They no longer have to rely on other professionals to get their work done. They can do so easily on their own computer set. Also, the data generated is accurate and you get many options to modify it. However, one also tries to learn M language. This is not necessary but knowing it will only increase the skill set.

M language is used in the coding of PowerQuery. So, if you know M language, you can also create custom functions for the PowerQuery for your data usage.

2.1 Installing power query

Pre-requisites for installing power query:

1. MS Office 2013 Professional Plus

2. Office 365 ProPlus

3. Excel 2013 standalone

4. MS Office 2010 Professional Plus with Software Assurance

You need to have any one of these.

2.2 Step by Step way to install Power Query

1. Go to https://www.microsoft.com/en-us/download/details.aspx?id=39379&CorrelationId=80a61fd2-635f-4fb9-acf2-7fdcae613ebb

2. In the end of the page, you will get download icon. But, you should first read the details, system requirements, install instructions and related resources. This will allow you to smoothly install power query.

3. After clicking download, you will get a screen like this:

4. Select the version you wish to download by ticking in the box.

5. Now, click on next button.

6. Open the setup wizard icon and install the power query.

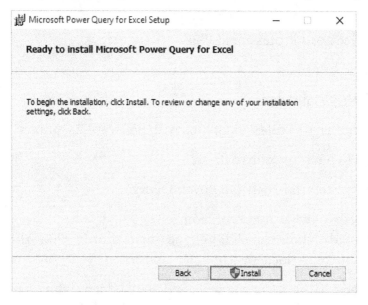

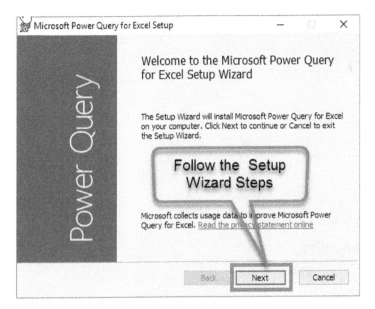

7. Now go to file menu and click on options.

8. Click on add-ins tab

9. Select COM Add-Ins from manage combo box.

10. Select Microsoft Power Query Preview for Excel from COM Add-Ins.

11. Power query tab appears in excel and is ready to be used.

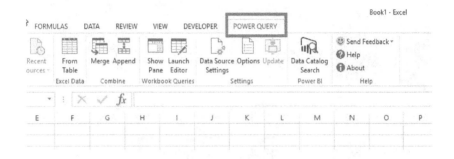

Chapter 3

Query sharing

What is query sharing?

People often construct various queries regarding their business in Excel. It could be for sales figures, profit and loss and so on. These sets of data may be merged for a new query. These queries are useful for other employees for the company and even serve as an online resource. Their collection and analysis are usually time-taking. Hence, it is wiser to share them for others to use. When the queries constructed are shared this way, it is known as query sharing.

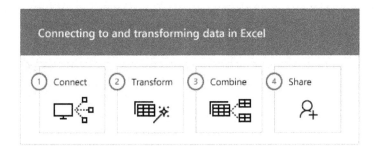

It is very common for the companies to use the older queries for training their new staff. In the absence of this query sharing feature, it was really difficult for the new employees to understand the tits-bits of this technology. But, query sharing also acts as a training material by storing every step of the operation.

Trainees or new employees can learn by studying every subsequent step just with a few clicks. Hasn't PowerQuery changed the face of the business analytics by making it time-efficient, error-proof and also as a training material?

How power query helps in query sharing?

Power Query saves the data, steps involved in acquisition and analysis and also the generated report in the power query formula language. In short, it automates the whole process involved in query creation. These steps can be easily accessed through the advanced editor tab under the view tab.

3.1 Sharing a query in Power Query

In order to share your query with others in the Power Query, you need to follow these simple steps:

1. Sign in to Power BI for Office 365 in MS-Excel.

2. Select the table or data that you wish to share.

3. Click on the query tab that is on the right side of the screen.

4. Now, click on share.

5. Now the shared query will appear in search results when any user online searches for this query.

3.2 How to import data from external sources?

There are times when you would need data from various sources. It could be from the Azure database of your own company or some online databases. You can use Power Query to import data from all sorts of external sources quite conveniently. The steps are as below:

1. Open MS-Excel home page.

2. Click on data icon

3. Choose the source from which you want to import data.

4. "From access" allow you to import data from MS-Access Database.

5. "From web" lets you to import data from the web.

When you click this icon, you will get a dialogue box to fill in the web URL you wish to visit. After that, click on import.

6. By choosing "from text", you can import data from a text file.

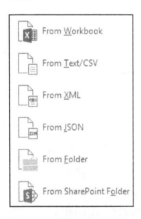

7. "From other sources" allows you to import data from other data sources that are:

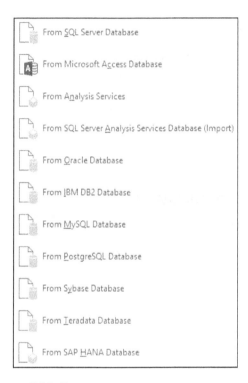

a. SQL Server

b. Analysis Services

c. XML data import

d. Data connection wizard & OLEDB

e. Microsoft query wizard & ODBC

8. If you select "existing connections", you will get a list of your commonly used data sources to choose from.

3.3 Understanding Query Editor

Query Editor enables you to modify and operate various data-related operations over a data source. You can add or subtract data tables and/or data types. You can perform various addition-deletions to rows and columns too. Query Editor creates instructions for these operations in the M language.

Power Query Editor Window
These buttons automate common processes!

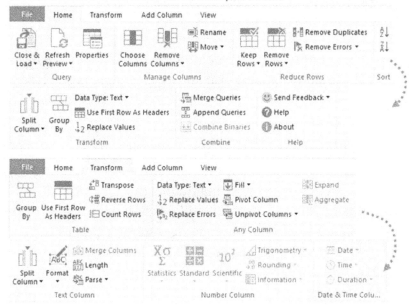

Query editor is an integral part of the Power BI and hence of the power query. Most of the data analysts use this part for the achieving the desired manipulations of the data acquired from various sources.

The language of the Query Editor

The programming language behind the power query is Power Query Formula Language, also known as M language. Here, M represents Data Mashup or Data modelling. It is a mashup query language.

Like all other programming languages, it has got its own set of structure and syntax. Because it is currently new and not so wide-spread, people usually maintain a distance from it. Additionally, its use for editing in Power Query which is itself a new program right now adds to the skeptics. But, as a matter of fact, this is a easy to understand with pretty easy syntaxes. Here we will explain the different components of the M language.

M's syntax:

M language consists of two programming blocks namely LET expression block and In expression block.

M language has different function categories. Some of them are:

- Date functions

- Error handling

- List functions

- Duration functions

- Accessing data functions

- Combiner functions

- Action functions

- Uri functions

- Splitter functions

- Logical functions

- And so on...

Chapter 4

Functions using Query Editor

Suppose you have procured a set of data from the internet that consists of several columns and rows. But, you have different needs. Like, you need data from only two rows and columns and wish to merge data from another table. All these functions can be easily performed in the Query editor.

Query editor has got distinct functions for rows and columns. Let us have a look over both of them individually.

4.1 Column Functions

When you have a data set, you may need to add, delete or modify the columns of it. Power query enables you to

a. Delete columns

b. Split or merge columns

c. Add custom columns

d. Sort and filter columns

e. Analyze cumulative data

f. Unpivot available data for pivot tables

To do that, you need to follow these steps:

1. Go to Power Query

2. Select edit; it will automatically take you to Query Editor.

3. In the Home tab, you get "manage columns."

a. You can choose columns here

b. You can delete one or more columns by selecting "remove columns."

c. You can rename a particular column by selecting "rename."

d. You can change the position of a particular column by using "move" option.

4. Under "transform", you will find different set of functions.

a. You can sort the columns according to a particular criterion by using "group by". This can be particularly helpful when you are dealing with different types of tables and wish to find some pattern in them.

b. You can also pivot or unpivot columns here.

c. You can split column(s) by selecting the option.

5. Under the "add column", you can find the below options:

a. You can custom create a column to include the data of your interest

b. You can also add an index column to keep track of your rows' numbers in the data.

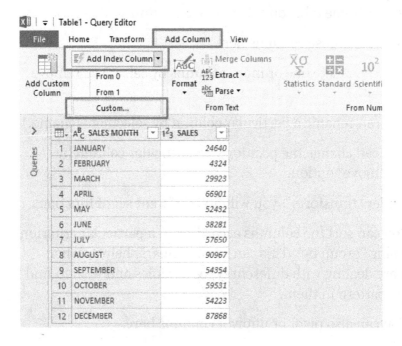

c. Using "duplicate column", you can create a copy of selected column(s).

d. You can also merge two or more columns by selecting "merge columns" option.

e. If you wish to change the format of your column, you can do so by selecting "format".

4.2 Row Functions You can also perform many functions with the rows in your data. Most of them work in the same way as the column functions. Here, we have explained them in steps.

1. Go to home tab in power query

2. Choose the desired function under the reduce row ribbon.

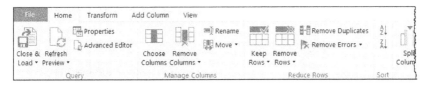

3. Under transform tab, you can do following operations:

a. Use the first row as the header in the data

b. Transpose, reverse and count rows

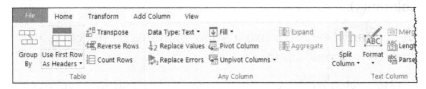

4.2 Transforming a query

When you are dealing with large datasets, you never know how you may have to shape the data to make them worth your use. As for example, you have a table that shows the year, production cost, profit, employee number, employee salary and expenses of a company. However, you need to work with only employee number and employee salary. All other columns are of no use to you. So, you need to delete them.

You can perform many other functions in a similar way. Let us give you an example:

1. Select PowerQuery tab.

2. Select get external data; select from the file; select excel.

3. You will get a list of excel files on your system.

4. Now, select the one on which you want to perform the operation.

5. When you select that, a navigator pane will open on the right side of the screen.

6. Select the table which you want to reshape.

7. Then select edit.

8. The query editor will appear on the screen as a pop-up window.

9. Select the properties that you want to change.

10. After making changes, click on close and load.

11. The changes made by you will appear in the new query.

In these simple steps, you can reshape the way data is presented in the tables. You can make the presentation more crisp and to-the-point. And at the top of it, all the relationship will be correctly established.

4.3 Refreshing a query

There are times when the tables or the query generated need to be updated constantly. Like, if you have made a query on a particular facebook page visits, then this statistic will change every hour. Many companies like the online shopping sites, have to keep a close watch on the number of visits on their website. Such sites derive their income from them. But, it will be very tedious process if someone needed to update the query every hour. Also, the chances of error will be high.

To prevent such errors and time-loss, there is a feature called refresh query in the query editor. All you need to do is put the function required and then refresh it. Any new data added or updated will be automatically updated in this query.

the simple steps;

1. Go to query editor

2. Click refresh preview

3. The query will be automatically updated

4.4 Filter a table

, get some undesirable data. Even useless data need to be filtered out for a good PowerQuery excel sheet. Else, it will become very confusing to look at even the un-related rows and column in the excel sheet. There are several options to filter a column. We have explained some of them briefly here;

1. Text filter: This is very much similar to find option. You can sort out the text data by filtering them with the words they contain or lack. Like, if there are many words beginning with R but you want to find those which don't begin with R, then you can put the text filter as: not beginning with R. All such words will automatically get sorted out. The steps involved are:

a. Select the column(s) to be filtered.

b. Select the down arrow at the top of the column name

c. Select "text filters".

d. You will get a menu containing filter options:

Equals

Does not equal

Begins with

Does not begin with

Ends with

Does not end with

Contains

Does not contain

e. Select the filter you wish to apply.

f. Select OK.

g. Text filter will sort out the text data according to the filter applied.

2. Auto filter

If you want to just default filter the columns of your table, you can select the auto-filter option. It can be applied in following ways;

a. for apply the auto-filter

b. There is a down arrow just beside the column name. Click it.

c. Select the auto-filter values that you want to apply.

d. Select OK.

e. Your query will be filtered according to the filters applied by you.

3. Number or date/time filters

Suppose you own a café. You want to monitor the time and day when your café has the highest footfall. For this, you need to have the number of customers that visited your café on a particular day. You can easily get the time and date and subsequently the number from your bill database. Now, you need to sort out the number of people present on a particular day and at a particular time.

For such scenarios, PowerQuery has a different filter that sorts out the columns according to number, date and time. Let us see the steps in which you can use this feature:

a. Select the column over which you want to apply this filter.

b. Select the down arrow.

c. Among the options that you will get, select number filters or date/time filters.

d. Click OK.

e. The filter will give you the analysis of how many people visited your café on a particular day.

f. You can also have a comparative study by clicking on the equality type filter. You can then make out the days on which you have maximum and minimum customers.

4. Filter column(s) by row position

When you deal with external data sheets, you get several unwanted rows. As for example, you have a data-sheet for past 10 years but you need only for the last 2 years. In this case, you have to filter out the top 8 rows. However, this may not always be the case. To make this easier, there are many customized options in the PowerQuery. You have following options for filtering rows:

a. Keep top 100 rows

• Select the table icon

• Select keep top 100 rows.

• Top 100 rows from your data sheet will be filtered out.

b. Keep top rows: Here, you have to manually enter the number of rows from the top to keep.

• Right click on the table icon.

• You will get a dialog box

• Select keep top rows option.

• Enter the number of rows from top which you want to keep.

• The filter will sort out the top X number of rows.

c. Remove top rows: It is helpful when you have smaller number of unwanted rows to remove. The steps involved are:

• Right click on the table icon.

• You will again get a dialog box demanding number of rows to be removed.

• Enter the number of rows that you want to remove.

• Always pay attention that this instruction says remove top rows. You should always fill in the number of rows from the top.

d. Remove alternate rows: Suppose you want to have data for the alternate years or months or whatever columns. Manually removing the alternate rows can be a tiring process. To make this work easier, you should use "remove alternate rows" option. The steps involved are:

• Right click on the table icon.

• Select "remove alternate rows".

• You will get a dialog box.

• In this box, fill in the first row number to be removed, total number of rows to be removed and also the total number of rows to keep. This ensures that wrong sequence of rows is not deleted. Also, when you count the total number of rows to be kept and removed, it helps you in tracking the filtered rows.

e. Keep range of rows: sometimes you may need to sort out the rows according to their range. This feature comes handy then. The steps involved are:

• Right click on the table icon.

• Select keep range of rows.

• You will get a dialog box demanding ranges to be kept.

• Enter the first row number and the total number of rows to be kept.

• Select OK.

• The filter will sort out the data according to the range you have applied.

There are several other functions that can be performed by the query editor. The other notable functions are:

• Sort a table according to different criteria or in ascending or descending order.

• Group rows of a table according to their values into a single row.

• Get cumulative data from table(s) for analyzing group operations like addition, subtraction.

• Expand a column that contains the required table

• Insert a custom made column into a table

• Merge several queries to create a new query

• Edit steps of query in advanced editor. You should know M language for performing this.

• Split columns

• Insert a new query into the excel worksheet

• Remove selected column(s) from a query... and the list goes on.

PowerQuery basically has all the functions' options that are needed by the analysts.

4.5 Utilizing Query Editor

Today there are several multi-national firms in the market. Together with that, even the small and medium scale businesses are trying to automate their whole process. This saves them with time and also manpower. The work which previously needed three to four accountants can now be finished in half the time by anyone well-versed in power query. This has accelerated the business operations and increased the efficiency of the work-force. Also, the companies are now able to get better data stats in lesser manpower.

Query editor is actually more than just an editor. You can perform a whole lot of functions to improve the data that you have collected.

Get proper manipulations in a meaningful manner and with absolutely zero errors. The best part of query editor is that anyone with the sound knowledge of MS-Excel can perform all the operations.

You can also use R programming language in query editor for further data cleansing and more sophisticated data output.

The only tricky part for the novices can be inserting functions. This requires practice. Also, if you want to customize the query instructions, you need to know the M language.

Chapter 5

Power Pivot

Power Pivot is basically an analytical tool (SQL Server Analysis Services Engine) for polishing the data received from power query. It was first introduced in Excel 2010 as an add-in. It can perform operations on millions of rows in a single excel sheet at once. And the best part is that these data can be from different sources. So, you can import any kind and any number of data from facebook or twitter and simultaneously perform various manipulations and analysis in a single excel sheet. We can say that is basically the upgraded version of excel. Excel can't handle this amount of data in the single sheet. Using power pivot, you can:

a. Establish a relationship between different tables

b. Arrange them in gradations

c. Establish properties of rows and columns

d. Create "key performance indicators."

e. Add suitable formulae with data analysis expressions.

Data Analysis Expressions (DAX) is the programming language used for Power Pivot. Anyone who uses power BI should know Power Pivot. Especially those who are involved in the data analysis field should learn it for their own use.

However, Power Pivot is available built-in only in Excel 2013 & 2016. If you wish to install Power Pivot add-in, you should follow these steps:

1. Go to file in Excel

2. Select options

3. Select Add-ins.

4. You will get a managed box; in its drop-down menu select COM Add-Ins.

5. Click go.

6. Tick mark the box that states "Microsoft power pivot for excel".

7. Click OK.

5.1 Merge Query

Suppose you have prepared two tables for your garment company. One table contains the total cost of production in last ten years along with profits earned. Another table contains the areas where your company has showed the maximum growth. Now, you wish to merge both these tables to establish the relationship between the profits and new market area gained by your company.

Many times, you get two large data sets that have one or two columns of your interest. But manually extracting data from those four columns can be very time-taking and prone to human errors. You can simplify the task by using merge function of the power query. It allows you to select the columns for merger and merges them very conveniently. You will get a new query that will contain columns from both the tables merged to give you the perfect set of data needed.

You can easily perform this using the "merge query" tab. You can perform two types of merges:

a. Intermediate merge: With each merge performed, a new query will be generated.

b. Inline merge: Using this, you can merge the whole table into your table. You can continue doing this until you reach your desired result.

Here, we will explain in steps, how to perform a merge:

1. Go to power query tab.

2. Select "merge" under the combined tab.

3. You will get a dialog box on your screen.

4. Select the primary table for merge from the drop-down list. Usually, the active query is taken as the primary table.

5. Select a column from the column header

6. Selected the secondary table or the table that you wish to merge with the first one.

7. Select the column from the column header that matches with this table.

8. When you are making multiple merges, you need to make sure that the number of columns selected in the primary and secondary (relatable) tables is same. If not, an additional dialog box will appear informing you of a failed merge.

9. Select "only include matching rows" to include only intersecting rows from both the tables. If you fail to tick this dialog box, all the rows from the primary table will get included in the resultant query. This may not always be desirable.

10. Click "OK".

11. You get a new query created out of the data from both the tables.

This can be performed in another way too. The steps are:

12. Go to power query tab

13. Click on the "show pane" option

14. Right-click on the "orders" query

15. Select reference from the list of options

16. This will create a new query. Right-click on the new query and select "edit".

17. Select the "merge" button in the power query editor.

18. The selected tables will be merged.

However, the earlier explained method is more convenient.

5.2 Multiple Joins (Vlookup)

Vlookup is basically for performing look-up function. Like a phone directory, it sorts out data in a particular pattern. Following that pattern, you can easily find the data you need. You need to enter the vlookup() in functions bar to get the unknown data that you want to extract from the set of available data.

Using power pivot, you can also merge multiple tables. The only requirement for this is to create a meaningful relationship between the columns of the multiple tables.

Here are the steps to perform multiple joins in power pivot using Vlookup.

1. Select the excel cell where you wish to have the desired value.

2. Write =Vlookup() in functions row.

3. Fill the parenthesis as (column where the desired result is needed, a range of cells containing data that you search, column number, true/false). Always put comma and colon between the values. Otherwise, Vlookup does not process the function.

4. Put false to get an exact match and true for an approximate match. True is the default option.

5. Press enter.

Points to be noted:

a. While putting a range, always put the colon between the two values. Like, if the look up value begins from the B2 cell and lasts in F12, then your range should be B2: F12. The absence of colon will not allow the function to run.

b. Always ensure that the data in the first column of the table array is a not a text. Otherwise, the function will return an error message.

c. Always use absolute references for range-lookup.

There is another way for merging columns. The steps are:

1. Select the Excel workbook

2. Navigate to the column you want to merge

3. Select merge from query tab

4. You will get a dialog box

5. Select the primary table()the one with the value you want to keep

6. Then select the relatable query

7. You will get a new expandable column.

8. Select organizational from the privacy levels dialog box.

9. This will give your both data sources, privacy.

10. Select save.

11. Select OK

12. Both the tables will be merged. And, you will get a new query with both the merged columns.

5.3 How is power pivot different from excel?

Till now, we have seen that the functions performed by power pivot are more or less similar to the functions performed by the excel. So, why is there so much emphasis on learning power pivot when we already are very comfortable with Excel?

Actually, both of these programs may seem similar but there are some basic differences between the two. In order for you to appreciate the importance of both of these separately, you need to know the difference that puts them apart.

The difference can be observed in the programming language of both of them and their syntaxes.

Power pivot functions always need some argument that consists of expressions or tables or values. These functions always begin with a = sign and are followed by any scalar expression. This scalar expression can be +, -, * and so on. Usually, Excel language utilizes arrays or sets of values as functions but power pivot utilizes tables and inputs for the same function.

In Excel, you can perform functions on particular cells or columns separately. You don't need to perform the function on the entire table or column. But, in the case of power pivot, you need to include the entire column or table in operation.

Chapter 6

Conditional Functions

PowerQuery works with a set of functions that are case sensitive. Also, they need to be filled in a particular pattern. Otherwise, you will get a null result. "If" is lowercase in PowerQuery and should not be confused with "IF" of excel.

Here we have explained how to perform PowerQuery if statements.

1. Go to query editor.

2. Select add column tab.

3. Now select the conditional column.

4. Fill up the new column name.

5. Fill up the subsequent fields.

6. Click OK.

We will be explaining important functions here.

6.1 Expression functions

You may need to deal with text values for many of your queries. They are usually tricky to handle. Here is a list of the expression functions that will help you to handle them.

a. Expression. Identifier: This can be used to get a text value that can be further used as an identifier from a text value.

b. Expression. Evaluate: This function analyses a text value and returns the result.

c. Expression. Constant: This returns a constant literal text from the value.

6.2 Table Functions

M language is used for scripting the functions in PowerQuery. In PowerQuery, tables are the backbone of the data. But you may need to perform certain operations on them to make them meet your needs. You have to just insert the proper function in the box. Here, we have mentioned some table functions for reference.

1. For table construction:

a. Table. View: This creates or extends a table according to the handlers defined by the user and also the customized action operations.

b. Table.FromRecords: This function lets a table to be returned from a list of data.

c. Table.FromColumn: This forces a table to return from a list that consists of nested lists and also the names and values of the columns.

2. For information on the tables:

a. Table.RowCount: This counts the number of rows in a table.

b. Table.Schema: This gives a new table that contains the column description of the selected table.

c. Table.ColumnCount: This counts the number of columns present in a specified table.

3. For conversions in tables or of the tables:

a. Table.ToRecord: This function gives a list of records from an input table as the output.

We have similar functions for table information, row operations and column operations.

Chapter 7:

Examples

We have explained enough of various functions of PowerQuery. Now, let us demonstrate how they work with two examples. In the first example, we have explained how to make an invoice data even the small businesses can benefit too much from using PowerQuery. They can plan strategically and can get an expert like income sheets to attract the investors.

In the second example, we have given an example of payroll statement. It is very common for the companies to project the growth of their employees in a fixed duration of time.

7.1 Invoice data

What is invoice data?

. Invoice data is actually the data that you get along with an invoice. PowerQuery actually works to extract the useful set of information from these invoices. As for example, a company generated 50 invoices in a month. Now, these invoice generation mean that the company managed to sell its 50 products in that particular month. You can now derive the profit gained for that month. With other PowerQuery tools, you can compare0-contrast them with other months. You can also predict the market growth scenario. Just by using PowerQuery you get a whole new field to play.

Here are the steps of creating invoice data using PowerQuery:

1. Open the excel sheet from which you want to generate the data.

2. Now select PowerQuery.

3. Select the columns you want to generate invoice from.

4. Select transform.

5. Select group by.

6. In the dialog box generated, fill the group by part with the distinguishing feature you need to use. It could be sales year or total profit; anything from the datasheet.

7. Fill in the new column name

8. Select operation from the drop-down menu.

9. The operations are the sum, average, median, minimum, maximum, count rows, count distinct rows and all rows.

10. Select the one that you need to perform.

11. Select the column option. You will get options to choose from the columns that you had selected in step 3.

12. Select ok.

13. You will get a unique list.

14. Go to the home tab.

15. Select close and load to option.

16. You will get a dialog box giving you options for loading columns.

17. Select load to a table.

18. Then select new worksheet.

19. Click load.

20. You will get a separate invoice data which you can even merge with the original data.

7.2 Payroll Statement

Suppose you have ten employees working for you. You have their monthly salary statements. Now, you want to estimate their salary growth for next 24 months. How will you do it?

Here, are the steps to perform this interesting task in PowerQuery:

1. Open the excel sheet with employees' names and current salary.

2. Add a column that states "increase" and add expected percentage increase under it.

3. Fill in the cells with expected salary after performing the required function in the function tab.

4. Perform the above-mentioned steps for each of the ten employees.

5. Now you get a query table.

6. Go to query editor.

7. Under query settings, fill in the name column.

8. In your case, it should be monthly salary.

9. Choose applied steps.

10. You will get three options:

a. Unpivot other columns

b. Renamed columns

c. Changed type 1

11. Choose category option from the screen

12. Choose unpivot other columns from the drop-down menu

13. Now choose attribute column.

14. Select rename columns from the query settings.

15. Rename attribute to month. You will get a numerical value for each of the months.

16. Select monthly increase query and refresh it.

17. Rename the second table generated.

18. In the functions column, write

=Table.RowCount(monthly increase)

19. Create a custom column by putting in the following instruction:

=List.Generate(() =>

[Month = 0, Salary125],

Each [Month]

Each [Month=[Month] + 1,
Salary=[Salary]*(1+MonthlyIncrease{[Month=[Month]+1]}[
Value])])

20. You will get a customized column.

21. Go to the home tab.

22. Now select manage parameters and then new parameters.

23. Give a new name to the parameter and fill in the other columns like put decimal in the value option.

24. When you change the parameter, you can also change the function from the drop-down menu.

25. Select create function. It will appear in the drop-down menu when you will select the new query generated.

26. Select OK.

27. Now, select add column.

28. Select 'invoke the custom function.'

29. You will get a dialog box. Fill in the new column name, function query and fill in the other details.

30. Click OK.

31. You will get a list which you can expand to new rows.

32. You will get the desired table.

The significance of PowerQuery in both these examples

Both these examples depict a typical usage of power query for performing business-related analytics. It can be seen from the example that how power query helps any business organization for performing certain analysis, specific to their need helping them to reach informed and accurate decisions.

Power Query is a tool which is the answer to all those scenarios which in its absence would have taken much more time and effort reaching the same conclusion. In the first example, a cafe owner was able to analyze the number of people who visited his shop in the entire month. He is now able to make much-informed decisions.

For example, he found that he had maximum foot-fall on Sundays between 4 pm-7pm. Now, he can arrange for more staff for this time slot that would cater to the needs of the customers. Also, he can arrange for more sitting area for these 3 hours. To attract even parents with kids, a small crèche inside the cafe will be perfect.

More coffee flavours and some discount for this limited time will be the perfect attraction for many. All these will ultimately lead to weigh more profit than he was previously making. All of this can be attributed to one informed decision of his. That is using power query to analyse the customer flow for an entire month.

Just imagine the effect that this kind of analysis and the subsequent informed business decisions can have on bigger and multi-national companies. pave the way for companies, big or small, are pitching for the inclusion of artificial intelligence software for their operational functions.

Chapter 8

Advance Features of Power Query

Advance feature of power query enables the user to write complex queries according to their need. You can use power query to create advanced queries. These queries use the power query formula language which can be used to build complex operations. Given below is the image depicting option from where this advance feature of power query can be used.

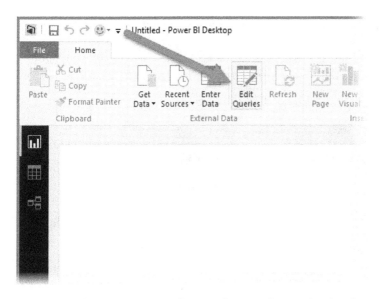

Here are the steps to perform advanced queries in the PowerQuery:

1. Go to data tab.

2. Select get data

3. Select from other sources.

4. Select blank query

5. Select query editor

6. Now, select the advanced editor.

7. You will get a note-pad like a screen showing the existing query code. You can change the codes to customize the editor.

8. PowerQuery uses M language. So, you need to be well versed in it.

9. After you have finished the coding, click on done.

10. Now, select a file from query editor menu.

11. Select close and apply.

12. Your code will be applied to the queries.

8.1 Scope of PowerQuery

With each passing day, the business organizations are moving from brick and mortar structures to online spaces. This we space provides them with a vast area to explore without the red-tape associated with traditional business enterprises.

These days, we get lots of people who are looking into the field of data analysis as their career. As a matter of fact, in the coming times, many career options will become obsolete just because of the increased role of data analysts. Big Data and Artificial intelligence is the key to the future.

With PowerQuery, one gets command over Big Data lying in the large pool called the internet. Extracting data associated with anything is now very easy. All you need to know is any Big Data programming like Hadoop or azure. After that, you can extract data from whatever field you wish.

But only data extraction can never be the key to success. One also needs to properly compile and refine them to suit the needs. What will a garment industry do with the data related to automobile tires? Nothing! Exactly, in the same way, one needs to sort out the data of use and discard the ones that are of no significance.

PowerQuery allows this refinement and manipulation of the data. You can create several new queries from a single table to cater to your different needs. If you wish to operate on only some parts of the data-sheets, you can easily delete rows and columns. If you are familiar with the M programming language, you can even make customized query functions.

According to the recent trends in the market, being unfamiliar to the PowerQuery will prove to be career limiting. As a matter of fact, many people are simply now unsuitable for IT jobs because of their unfamiliarity with the Big Data and Artificial Intelligence software.

Those who are familiar to the PowerQuery can present a well-organized and nicely analyzed data. This is always a big demand for all the firms. So, how exactly PowerQuery leads to a well-organized data? Here are the few points:

a. You can find and merge the same data accumulated from different sources. Thus, you will get rid of duplicates.

b. You can edit the faults in the data and put the correct values. This will simply eliminate the confusion arising out of different values for the same data.

c. You can even create customized queries to suit your different needs.

d. You can perform several edits, sorts, renaming and likewise functions on whatever number of tables you wish to do.

People need to come out of the mentality that Excel has got limited functions. Today, it has got more functions than any specialised data analytics tool. The efficiency and accuracy provided by PowerQuery are unmatched. And, the only thing that one needs to learn separately is M language. I would suggest that people should learn it for making maximum utilization of PowerQuery. It will also enable them to be more efficient with their data analytics task.

Who should use power query?

People are way too much confused about the usage of power query. Ask anyone and they would ask you back that why they should use power query when they are already using excel. Now, they need to be explained that power query is not a replacement of excel. In fact, it is an add-in of it. In other words, power query is an extension of the excel for its more efficient handling of a large amount of data.

So, who should use it more often?

a. Anyone involved with business decision making. These people need to deal with the unusually large amount of data that expands over a wide field. If they are not provided with any artificial intelligence software to ease their work, their true potential will be consumed in manually handling the data.

If these people will use Power Query, they will be able to extract a large amount of refined data from the web space. Their analysis and further course of action will be much in sync with the market demand.

Ultimately, the company will benefit. Otherwise, if these data analysis function will be performed manually, it would mean more time taken and also more chances of human errors. These can severely lower the quality of the analysis. But, software like power pivot can ease these complexities and pave way for more concise yet precise data.

b. Anyone dealing with incorrect data: Not only business analysts, even the small businesses are nowadays using data analytics tools to further expand their business. These establishments may not always have a proper business analyst. But owing to the user-friendly interface of power query, anyone fluent with the MS-Excel can easily handle the data analytics.

They can utilize these tools for editing the wrong queries and even for editing the data sheets to suit their needs.

If a firm needs data on the population of a place and number of bread packets consumed, they can conveniently delete the columns that depict consumption of flour and rice. This seamless editing capacity allows every business owner to get a better grasp of the data of their company.

They can use it for their business outlook and better decision making.

c. A newbie in the IT field: Newbies need to keep themselves equipped with the latest technologies to attract the recruiters most.

Learning power query is the best shot for them right now. They will be able to analyze and modify the company's data very efficiently.

Since Power Query is what we can call artificial intelligence and big data combined; it is going to affect for a very long time. In fact, even the experienced IT professionals should learn it. It would help them in easing their workload and also in remaining updated with the recent technologies.

Future of power query

The pace at which artificial intelligence and big data are ruling the current world is simply incredible. The best example can be seen when you move from one region to another. When you see a YouTube video, you must have noticed that there are advertisements.

You will be surprised to notice that these advertisements are always according to the region in which you currently are. You will never get advertisements in German when you are in New York - unless, of course, you are from Germany - in which case, Google manages to tailor product offerings that might interest you - even in German.

Your smartphone tracks your position and updates it, and if advertisers choose geo specific locations to advertise, you wouldn't get German ads while in New York.

Every company has now got data analysts pitching for their product in every possible way. Youtube advertisements are also a part. When it is detected that you are in an English speaking region, it begins to show you advertisements in

English - even if you do not know that language. Nothing can escape the attention of careful data analysts and their equally efficiently programmed analysis tool.

With such a vast effect on how we carry out business, the Power Query is definitely the pillar of future data analytics. It will allow anyone and everyone concerned with collection, study, analysis and interpretation of data. It will allow the business decision makers to experiment any new product or scheme with minimum risk.

With better access to accurate data, businesses can make the right decisions and leverage in on growth faster. That's one reason startups can't ignore the Power Query.

They can even garner more revenue just from the likes, comments and shares from the social networking sites. It can be comfortably said that the rise of power query will lead to the sleeper success phenomenon where many companies may not be in direct profit through the sale of their products but in indirect profits through their catchy advertisement campaigns.

As for the traditional business enterprises, power query will prove to be a boon. Currently, the role of data analysts or business analysts is much limited. They are concerned only with the decision making. But in the coming time, they will have a bigger role to play.

They can pitch for better advertisement campaigns through a well-documented research on the likes and dislikes of the population; can work in the hiring process by sorting out the candidates based on their LinkedIn profiles and the list is endless. The magnitude of change that power query is going to bring is unlimited.

As for example, we all know that LinkedIn and Glassdoor are currently the best online job portals. Now, if a company wishes to find best candidates for its job position, it can also employ power query here.

The data will be edited and polished in the query editor to meet the company requirements. Candidates can be sorted out on the basis of their educational qualifications and previous experience just like the normal edits. This will leave the company with a list of best candidates to be hired. The time and expenditure that was earlier used in the whole recruitment process will be decreased by several times. Thus, power query will rule the recruitment world too.

Currently, there is an ever-growing percentage of companies that are pitching for more use of power query in their firm. As of a data source, currently, 45,000 companies are employing power query for better data collection, differentiation and analysis. This can free them from the hassles of installing separate servers and software. Many resources needed to be invested in their maintenance too.

The mobility of the employees was limited. But with the introduction of power query, all these factors have simply vanished. Companies do not need to maintain such expensive servers. All the information I snow stored in the cloud. This has led to more mobility of the employees. This is the reason that most companies now pitch for work from home option.

The best part of power query is that unlike previous data analytical tools that needed a specific programming language to be learnt for proper use, it is fit to be used even for a non-technical person. Except for the customized column creation feature, the whole of the power query is pretty user-friendly. It needs no extra knowledge of any programming or query language. Even a person with the basic knowledge of MS-Excel can sign into this tool and gain insightful views over the various online data sheets and use them for further analysis. Its outreach can be understood by its statistics itself. Nearly 1 million users around the world are currently using power query for various data analytical purposes.

Going by this figure, it will be a matter of a couple of years, which almost all the business enterprises will be utilizing power query for one or the other purpose.

One of the best user-friendly features that have been introduced in these data analytical tools is their mobile-friendly versions.

This allows the users to access the data from anywhere and then perform the required function with just a few touches. Its user-friendly version allows even the businessmen to access their business data sheets and derive the various outcomes without the help from any business analyst. This has in fact given them more control over their operations and certainly more freedom.

Power Query also allows for continuous refreshing of the data. It means that if you have put a function over a particular data sheet that changes after every transaction, then by simply clicking the refresh options, you can update the table. This feature is especially helpful for those who are involved in online businesses. Also, those who are operating facebook business pages or YouTube channels will benefit from this feature. Keeping track of the visitors on a facebook page or any other online platform is very tough. It changes every second and does not follow any particular pattern.

In such a scenario, manually entering the updated data after every hour will be very tedious and definitely susceptible to human errors. However, with the refresh query feature of power query, these can be handled efficiently.

Microsoft is continuously working to upgrade the data analytics for everyone who uses power BI. Since it is easily adaptable with azure HDinsight, Hadoop and many other Big Data programs, its use across the various platforms is highly projected. So anyone who wants to learn data analytics to gain more insight into their business operations should surely get familiar with Power Query. It is going to be the future of business operations.

--

Conclusion

Thank you again for downloading this book!

I hope this book was able to help you .

Finally, if you enjoyed this book, then I'd like to ask you for a favor, would you be kind enough to leave a review for this book on Amazon? It'd be greatly appreciated!

www.ingramcontent.com/pod-product-compliance
Lightning Source LLC
Chambersburg PA
CBHW071135050326
40690CB00008B/1474